A MESSAGE FROM THE NBWA

"The Financial Handbook for Next Generation Beer Wholesalers is an insightful resource that we are thrilled to offer to our members. It simplifies and demystifies beer finances for distributors of all shapes and sizes. Read this book. It will help you make smart decisions and improve financial results."

CRAIG PURSER,
President & CEO, NBWA

"I am so excited to get this book in our members' hands! Prior to NBWA, I worked as CFO for a beer distributor and wish this handbook had been available. Kary delivers practical and straightforward financial advice specifically targeted to beer distributors. I don't know anywhere else that you can find such targeted guidance. Make sure to get a copy in the hands of everyone on your finance team!"

KIMBERLY MCKINNISH,
Senior Vice President & CFO, NBWA

BEER BUSINESS FINANCE

A Handbook for the Next Generation

Kary Shumway, CPA

Beer Business Finance
Numbers are Friends, LLC
15 Spring Hill Road
Hancock, NH 03449
Website: www.BeerBusinessFinance.com
email: Kary@BeerBusinessFinance.com

CONTENTS

GROSS PROFIT

OPERATING EXPENSES

FINANCING AND LOAN BASICS

CASH FLOW MANAGEMENT

INVENTORY MANAGEMENT BEST PRACTICES

COMPENSATION PLANNING

WHOLESALER OPERATIONS

INTRODUCTION

MY JOURNEY IN THE BEER business started two decades ago. I was working at a CPA firm doing tax returns, financial statements, and audits. The local beer wholesaler, a client of our firm, had an opening for a CFO as the current one was retiring after 47 years. I was lucky enough to be offered the position.

During my first few years in the business, we transitioned from second to third generation of family ownership. Grandfather started the business, then dad took over, and now it was time for the sons to take the helm.

The family generations who came before did a remarkable job of building and growing the business. However, the market had changed. Gone were the days of high sales growth and low competition. Beer sales were slowing down while competition was speeding up.

We knew we had to change many areas of the business to keep pace with the changes in the market. We needed new technology, new training methods, and new skill sets as well as better financial processes and procedures to improve financial reporting and understand business performance.

It was time to get to work.

In this book, I provide a summary of the many things I learned as our beer business transitioned from one generation to the next. It's a compilation of the tips, tactics, and strategies that proved useful and profitable as we grew the business.

This book is for not only beer wholesalers who want to improve financial results in their business but also non-financial owners and managers who recognize they don't know enough about their business finances, but want to learn more.

Here's the thing: You understand your business; you know your market, your customers and your products better than anyone. The financial statements are simply the numerical representation of this knowledge. This book will help you make the connection between the business you understand and the financial numbers that measure results.

Maybe you want to reduce out of code beer expenses, gain control over inventory SKUs, or create incentive programs for your sales team to sell more beer. Maybe you want to learn tactics to increase gross profit, reduce operating expenses, and improve cash flow. Or maybe you just want to learn to read the financial statements a little better and understand what they are telling you.

If this sounds familiar, this book is for you. I will share what worked and what didn't so that you can learn from our successes as well as our failures.

Topics we will cover in detail:

- Strategies to grow sales in a hyper-competitive market
- Tools to manage and improve wholesaler gross profit

- Specific ideas and tactics to reduce operating expenses
- Templates and spreadsheet models to monitor and improve cash flow and profitability

The ideas and methods presented in the book are the ones I've used in the real world to help improve our beer distribution business. I hope they will do the same for you.

Let's get started.

HOW TO USE THIS BOOK

THIS BOOK PRESENTS SPECIFIC METHODS to improve financial results in your beer business. When you come across an idea that may work, write it down, and make a plan to take action. (When I read a book, I love to take notes. I write in the margins, highlight sections, and dog-ear the pages I want to come back to.)

At the end of each chapter is an Action Item page where you can add notes on what you learned and jot down ideas you want to implement in your business. The goal is to put the information in this book to use.

The methods detailed come with step-by-step instructions. However, if you get stuck or need more support, below are some resources that may help:

- Join the Beer Business Finance Membership. This gets you unlimited access to online courses, guides, and archived issues of the beer finance newsletter.
- Subscribe to "CFO in a Box." This one-on-one service provides you with customized guidance on how to achieve the financial results you want.

You can learn more about these resources at www.BeerBusinessFinance.com. Moreover, the references to spreadsheets, tools, and resources throughout the book are all available for download on the website.

Knowledge + Action = Results. Use the knowledge in this book and take action to improve your financial results. Your income statement is counting on you.

BEER FINANCES 101

INTRODUCTION TO BEER FINANCE

IT HAS BEEN SAID THAT business is a game and financial statements are the scoreboard. To determine whether you are winning or losing, you need to keep an eye on the scoreboard and understand the results. However, the financial statements or scoreboard for your beer business are a little more complicated than one you might see at a football game.

On the financial scoreboard are an income statement, balance sheet, and cash flow statement. There are also income, expense, gross profits and net profits, not to mention assets, liabilities, and equity. It's clear there's a lot going on with the financial scoreboard. It's hard to figure out which figure to look at and how to know if you're winning or losing.

To read the financial scoreboard, you need a little training in financial literacy or understanding how monetary transactions work. It is perhaps the most important business skill you can learn. Moreover, it's the most important one you can teach your employees.

WHY IS FINANCIAL LITERACY IMPORTANT?

When you become financially literate, you can read and understand the financial statements or scoreboard of your company performance. You gain new insight into the operating results. It's like having X-ray vision to see through the fog of the day-to-day business and answer basic financial questions: Why are sales down? Why are gross margins shrinking? Why are expenses going up?

Financial literacy opens your eyes to what is really going on in your company. It gives you the ability to see beyond the numbers and right down to the root cause of the problems.

WHY TEACH FINANCIAL LITERACY TO YOUR EMPLOYEES?

Financial literacy isn't just for owners and executives. Teaching it to your employees creates a culture of business people -- employees who understand how money works, how business works, and how to dramatically improve financial results.

Moreover, financial literary illustrates to employees that they do have an impact on the business. It shows them the connection between their efforts and the achieved results so they understand the significance of their work and importance of their contribution. After all, employees give a tremendous amount of their time, energy, and passion to the business, and they want to know they are making a difference.

In short, teaching yourself and your employees to become financially literate will transform your company.

CONCLUSION

To win the game of business, you need financial literary to understand the score. This chapter simplifies financial statements so that you can read them as easily as a football scoreboard.

ONE BENEFIT OF EACH FINANCIAL STATEMENT

"Numbers have life; they're not just symbols on paper."
- Shakuntala Devi

LET'S START WITH AN INTRODUCTION to three main financial statements: income, balance sheet, and cash flow statements. We'll review the information on each report and highlight one immediate benefit of reading them on a regular basis.

At the end of this section is a challenge. Should you accept, I guarantee you will experience immediate, positive financial results in your business.

FINANCIAL STATEMENT BASICS

The income, balance sheet, and cash flow statements are the Three Wise Men of financial reporting. You've probably heard of them, but let's get to know them a little better.

- Income statement: Also known as the P&L (Profit and Loss) statement, it tracks company revenue, gross profit, and expenses. To remember this, use the acronym REX for Revenue and Expense. The P&L shows us the mighty bottom line – whether we had a profit or a loss. Everybody loves the P&L; it's like the popular kid in high school.

- Balance sheet: It records assets, liabilities, and equity. Assets are what the company owns, liabilities are what the company owes, and equity is the difference between the two. To remember these items, think ALE for Assets, Liabilities and Equity.
- Cash flow statement: This financial document has the best name; everyone loves cash flow. Think of it like your checkbook. It shows money in and money out. While the income statement measures transactions, the cash flow statement measures the inflow and outflow of cash. Keep in mind profit and cash flow are two very different things.

ONE IMMEDIATE BENEFIT OF READING EACH FINANCIAL STATEMENT

1. P&L: See the Results of Operations. The primary purpose of the income statement is to tell us whether we had a profit or a loss. Pretty simple. The P&L shows you the results of the company operations for a period of time, usually the current month and the year to date. The main benefit of reading it is seeing the bottom line, but you knew that already.

2. Balance Sheet: Assess Company Net Worth. This statement provides much more than ALE or "nuts and bolts" information. In fact, it shows you the health of the company in the form of Net Worth, which is the equity. The higher this figure, the better the health of the company.

3. Cash Flow Statement: Understand the Net Change in Cash. What could be more important than knowing whether cash increased or decreased during the month or year to date? Read this statement to check your cash position and understand where the cash came from and where it went. Afterward, you can work on increasing the cash in and decreasing cash out. That's the kind of math we all like.

CONCLUSION

The first step to financial literacy is learning the basic components of the three key financial statements. You may only read the income statement as of now, but the balance sheet and cash flow statement provide vital information about your business. Don't deny yourself the delicious information the Three Financial Wise Men have to offer.

TAKE THE BEER DISTRIBUTOR FINANCE CHALLENGE

Now you have the What and Why of three financial statements, it's time to put this knowledge into action in your beer business. The challenge starts you on a path toward financial literacy.

- First, get a current copy of your income statement, balance sheet, and cash flow statement.
- Next, look over them and see if you can identify the items listed on each, e.g., income, expense, assets, liabilities, etc.
- Most importantly, look for the One Immediate Benefit as detailed above. What is the profit for the year? The company equity? The cash flow?

GENERAL LEDGER SIMPLIFIED

"Confusion, when embraced, is the starting point for discovery, direction and decision."

- Richie Norton

THE FINANCES OF YOUR BEER business can be confusing, no question about it. There are debits, credits, accruals and all sorts of weird accounting language that make it hard to understand the numbers. Regardless of the difficulty, you must learn to read and understand the financial statements so you can learn what is going on in the business.

Here's the secret: Learning to read and understand the financial statements is not that hard. You just need a guide (me), a few pointers and you'll be on your way to a solid understanding of your distributor finances.

In this section, we'll get back to basics and simplify beer business finances. The goal is to help you understand how your finances work so that you can gain control over them and improve financial performance.

BEER BUSINESS FINANCES: BACK TO BASICS

- A quick introduction to general ledger accounts: What they are and why you need them
- Basic financial reporting: How the general ledger gets organized
- Creating a book of simple financial reports to track your results

GENERAL LEDGER ACCOUNTS

The general ledger accounts are a detailed listing of all the things you want to track and measure in your business. Their purpose is to provide organization and structure for your financial reporting.

With your beer business, you need to track assets, liabilities, revenues, and expenses. For example, the general ledger will display assets like this:

- Cash
- Accounts Receivable
- Inventory

Each of the items above is a general ledger account under the Assets category on your financial statements.

To keep things organized, the accounting system puts a number in front of the general ledger account name. This makes it easier to group and sort the general ledger accounts. But the real reason is that the bean counters just really like numbers.

With the numbers in place, the general ledger accounts start to look like this:

- 1000-00 Cash
- 1200-00 Accounts Receivable (A/R)
- 1300-00 Inventory

The full listing of general ledger accounts is called a chart of accounts. It's not necessary to learn this terminology, but it does help to have a working knowledge so that you can communicate with the numbers people. They have a language all their own.

General ledger numbers have structure and meaning. For example, above is the number 1200-00 for accounts receivable. The 1200 may represent the base account (the accounts receivable), and the 00 may represent the department or business entity related to the A/R.

Don't get lost on this part. It's not important to grasp all of this right away, but it is useful to understand that general ledger accounts can be as simple or as complex as you want them to be. It all depends on the level of detail you want to track in your business.

ACTION ITEMS

Review the general ledger and chart of accounts in your beer business. This is the detailed listing of all the items that your accounting system is set up to track. Read through the information to get a feel for what is in there and what might be missing.

Ask a few questions to better understand your general ledger accounts:

- What is the account structure? Does it look like the 1000-00 noted above, or is it something different?
- Why is it set up the way it is? If you don't understand, find someone who does.
- Is there important information your general ledger accounts aren't capturing?

They should be a listing of everything you want to track in your business. If a category of assets, liabilities, revenues, or expenses is important to report on, it should have its own general ledger account.

Once you spend some time with your general ledger accounts, it won't take long before you start to feel comfortable and gain some confidence on how these things work. Then, you'll be ready to take the next step in the financial journey.

Next, we'll dig into Basic Financial Reporting and how the general ledger gets organized. Embrace the confusion as a starting point for discovery. Your beer business finances will thank you.

FINANCIAL REPORTING SIMPLIFIED

"I believe that through knowledge and discipline, financial peace is possible for all of us."

- Dave Ramsey

BY NOW, YOU UNDERSTAND THAT beer distributor owners and managers should learn to read and understand financial statements as it's the only way to know what's going on financially in the business. With this knowledge you can identify and fix problems that are costing you money as well as find opportunities to increase net income and put more cash in the bank account.

In the previous section, we simplified the general ledger. In this section, we'll simplify financial reporting. The goal is to help you understand how your finances work so you gain control, understand the results of the business, and improve financial performance.

BEER BUSINESS FINANCIAL REPORTING

- Financial reporting simplified
- The Big Three: Income statement, balance sheet, cash flows
- How to create a book of simple financial reports to track your results

FINANCIAL REPORTING SIMPLIFIED

Financial reporting is the process of producing statements that show the company's financial status to owners, management, investors and the government -- yes, Uncle Sam is very interested in your financial results as well. Its main objective is to provide useful information for decision-making. For example, the reports indicate whether the business is making a profit and also provide information on whether there's enough cash or borrowing ability to invest in new trucks, equipment or personnel.

The building blocks of the financial reports are the general ledger accounts. The latter represent the detailed listing of the items you want to track in your business. The financial reports summarize this listing into different forms known as the income statement, balance sheet, and statement of cash flow.

THREE KEY FINANCIAL REPORTS

Repetition is the mother of all learning, so let's briefly review the financial reports one more time. The income statement, balance sheet and statement of cash flow make up the traditional financial statements. Altogether, they present information on profitability, equity and most important, the company cash flow. You need all three to get a complete view of financial operations.

The income statement, also known as the P&L (profit and lost), tracks company revenue, gross profit, and expenses. Second, the balance sheet records assets, liabilities and equity. Third, the cash flow statement is like your checkbook – it shows money in and money out.

HOW TO CREATE A BOOK OF SIMPLE FINANCIAL REPORTS

It's useful to have a big picture understanding of financial reporting alongside a working knowledge of what each financial statement tells you. However, this stuff makes a lot more sense when you apply it to the numbers in your own beer business.

My recommendation to owners and managers is to keep the financial reporting as simple as possible to start. This way, you'll have the information you want without getting overwhelmed.

Simple financial reports are summarized financial reports. They show totals, instead of a lot of detailed numbers. They also present the numbers using metrics or ratios, which make the information easier to digest.

Keys to creating a simple book of financial reports:

- Use summarized information, instead of pages and pages of details
- Use metrics and ratios to simplify the information

- Organize and present the reports in a way that is meaningful to you. For example, if you want to see revenue per employee, or net income as a percentage of payroll, put that right on the report where you can easily see it.

Beer Business Finance				
Simple Distributor Income Statement				
For the Month Ended:	**30/06/2019**			
	Month - Actual	**Month - Budget**	**Year-to-Date Actual**	**Year-to-Date Budget**
Sales	$425,000	$400,000	$2,550,000	$2,400,000
Cost of Goods Sold	$315,000	$300,000	$1,890,000	$1,800,000
Gross Profit	$110,000	$100,000	$660,000	$600,000
Gross Profit %	26%	25%	26%	25%
Operating Expenses	$85,000	$70,000	$510,000	$420,000
Net Income (Loss)	$25,000	$30,000	$150,000	$180,000
Net Income (Loss) %	6%	8%	6%	8%

WRAP UP + ACTION ITEMS

Understand what the financial report tells you, and you can leverage them to make better decisions. Start with a review of your financial statements: income statement, balance sheet and statement of cash flow. Spend some quality time to get to know them.

Ask some basic questions like:

- What is net income for the month and year to date?

- What are total assets?
- What is cash flow for the year?

Ask some more detailed questions:

- What is net income per employee?
- Do we track net income for our different product lines (beer, non-alcohol, wine)?
- How do our results compare to industry averages?

The financial reports should provide the answers to the above as well as any other information you feel is important to run your business. Although there is no end to the type of financial reporting you can create, start with simple, summarized reports. You'll be simply amazed at the results.

FINANCE FOR NON-FINANCIAL MANAGERS

"The three great essentials to achieve anything worthwhile are: hard work, stick-to-itiveness and common sense."

-Thomas Edison

ACCORDING TO A BEER INDUSTRY study, 80 percent of wholesalers share some form of financial info with their management teams. The question is, does the latter know how to read it? And more importantly, do they know how to use it?

The financials tell a story, but the language is foreign to most everyone, except the bean counters. That's why, in this section, we'll explore a concept called finance for non-financial managers, also known as operational finance, and cover financial numbers meaningful to your sales manager and operations people.

Operational finance for non-financial managers presents the numbers in plain English so your managers can understand and use the information to improve financial results in your beer business.

It identifies and quantifies the most important functions in each department.

The first step to implement operational finance in your beer business is to individualize the finances by department. A typical beer distributor will have many (or all) of the departments listed below:

- Sales
- Merchandising
- Delivery
- Warehouse (day shift)
- Warehouse (night shift)
- Admin (Customer service, Accounting, HR, IT)
- Garage / Truck maintenance
- Facilities / Building maintenance

People understand functions, roles and responsibilities. They understand what they are supposed to do and how to do it. However, they don't always know how these activities can be quantified nor their impact on financial statements. The goal is to show your managers how to quantify and measure performance. Doing so gives them a tool to improve financial results.

The financials provide a representation of actions and decisions that employees make every day. Operational finance helps to measure and report on these actions and decisions on a departmental level.

Next, we'll look at specific metrics for each department. We'll also explore how these measurements (Critical Numbers) tie back to the financial statements. Before your non-financial managers realize what's happening, they'll be doing finance.

FINANCE FOR NON-FINANCIAL OPS MANAGERS

"The greatest teacher I know is the job itself."

James Cash Penney

ONE DAY, YOUR GENERAL MANAGER will understand how to read a full set of financial statements. Until that time, show them how to use operational finance. This concept focuses on the critical numbers your general manager should monitor to ensure the success of the business.

Traditional financial statements measure the results of the entire organization, while operational finance presents numbers on a more granular level individualized by department. In short, it offers a common-sense presentation of the numbers.

Critical numbers measure results; they are metrics that make a difference and define success in your beer business. Everyone should have a critical number and an easy way to measure performance in each department.

By definition, general managers have a lot of critical numbers to measure. The operations manager oversees many (or all) of the departments below:

- Delivery
- Warehouse (day)
- Warehouse (night shift)
- Inventory
- Facilities Maintenance
- Garage / Vehicle Maintenance

For each department it is necessary to have a critical number (or numbers) to measure success. Critical numbers are similar to key performance indicators, benchmarks or other key metrics you may have used before. The main difference is that critical numbers measure only the most important number and tie back to a specific area of the financial statements. Common sense critical numbers allow your GM to monitor financial information without having to understand how to read a balance sheet.

CRITICAL NUMBERS FOR OPERATIONS MANAGERS

Critical numbers quantify the work being done and use common sense language to report the results. They are meaningful and relevant to employees who are actually doing the work. Below is a sampling of critical numbers for operations managers:

- Delivery: cost per case delivered compared to gross profit per case, profit per stop, profit per route
- Warehouse (day shift): product rotation, cleanliness of warehouse, breakage vs. goal, number of trailers unloaded and put away

- Warehouse (night shift): cases picked per hour, picking accuracy, breakage, cleanliness at end of shift
- Inventory: days on hand, inventory turns, out of stocks, Inventory variances
- Maintenance: project accountability, securing multiple quotes for vendor work
- Garage: monitor/report on billable hours, accurate inventory levels for parts

The Ops manager is responsible for these numbers, which can be shared with other department managers for further oversight. For example, the delivery team leader should monitor profit per stop and profit per route, while the warehouse supervisor will monitor product rotation by the day shift, cases picked per hour, and accuracy of the night team. Each manager will have a critical number and an understanding of how the number is calculated.

Below is an example of a critical number scorecard for the warehouse picking team:

Night Loader Scorecard								
Picking Speed / Picking Accuracy								
Name: Joe Picker								
	Pallet Picks	**Case Picks**	**Bottle Picks**	**Total Picks**	**Hours**	**Cases per Hour**	**Mispicks**	**Accuracy Rate %**
Monday	6	580	-	586	9.5	61.68	7	98.8%
Tuesday	-	475	-	475	8.0	59.38	-	100.0%
Wednesday	2	750	-	752	8.5	88.47	-	100.0%
Thursday	1	1,020	-	1,021	10.0	102.10	4	99.6%
Friday	1	1,150	96	1,247	9.0	138.56	5	99.6%
Weekly Total	***10***	***3,975***	***96***	***4,081***	***45.0***	***90.69***	***16***	***99.6%***

WRAP UP + ACTION ITEMS

To teach finance to non-financial managers, you don't need to start with income and expense or assets and liabilities. It's all about providing common sense numbers to your department managers. These critical numbers measure the work being done, link back to the income statement, and make a real difference in improving financial results.

It's easy for your operations manager, delivery manager and warehouse manager to understand these critical numbers. Best of all, as they improve these metrics, they will also improve the financial results in your business. It's just common sense.

FINANCE FOR NON-FINANCIAL SALES MANAGERS

"We are what we repeatedly do. Excellence, then, is not an act, but a habit."

- Aristotle.

NEXT, WE'LL LOOK AT OPERATIONAL finance for your sales manager. And let's face it, no one in your company needs common sense financial training more.

The sales manager is the rainmaker of the organization. Without them, sales would shrink and the bank account would run dry. This employee impacts far more than just the sales line on the income statement.

To begin, let's cover the basic steps to teach finance to your non-financial sales manager so you increase profits as well as top line sales. Along the way, your sales manager will be shocked to learn there are more line items on the income statement besides sales!

OPERATIONAL FINANCE FOR SALES MANAGERS

I like to poke fun at sales managers because they are an easy target. In my experience working with dozens of sales managers over the years, I've seen only one or two who understood anything beyond the sales line on the income statement.

Nevertheless, the sales manager plays a vital role for the beer distributor. They have a tremendous amount of responsibility, and the decisions they make impact all aspects of the business. Moreover, they make decisions every day that affect profitability. Teach them to make better decisions using operational finance.

Just as with Ops manager, the first step to teach finance to non-financial sales managers is to present them with common sense numbers, ones that are meaningful and relate to the work they do every day.

CRITICAL NUMBERS FOR SALES MANAGERS

The sales manager has no shortage of numbers to track. The big breweries are famous for burying the sales manager in key performance indicators and metrics of all kinds. The problem is these metrics only measure the sales line on the income statement.

Two critical numbers to introduce to your sales manager are gross profit and cost to deliver.

GROSS PROFIT

Gross profit is the amount earned on each sale, not just the sales dollar, but the cost of the product sold. Many sales managers just don't know or haven't been taught this. Sales – Cost of Goods = Gross Profit.

Further, the gross profit percentage on sale is an easy way to indicate what percentage of the sale is gross profit. (Hint: It's not 100 percent). Gross Profit divided by Sales = Gross Profit Percentage (GP %)

In a typical distributor, the GP % is around 25 percent. This number has blown away every sales manager I've worked with in the past.

"You're telling me we only keep 25 cents on every sales dollar?"

They can't believe it. And they are shocked even more when we talk about the operating expenses required to support the sale. That leads us to the cost to deliver.

COST TO DELIVER

Gross profit indicates the net amount made on each sale, while the cost to deliver includes all the other expenses required to get the product on the shelf. It is an average of all the operating costs of the distributor: administration, warehouse, delivery, merchandising, etc. The number can be presented as a percentage of the sale price or as a set amount per case.

The sales manager can use cost to deliver as a basis for making decisions that affect profitability. For example, they may need to decide whether to make special deliveries or send out a hot shot, and they may also decide on price reductions or determining when to fire sale of products.

WRAP UP + ACTION ITEMS

No one in your organization needs financial training more than your sales manager. You know this in your heart to be true. Show your sales manager how to calculate gross profit, GP %, and average cost to deliver and set up simple reports they can use to track this information. With this knowledge, they are in position to help improve not only the sales line on the income statement, but also the gross profit and the bottom line. The results may be shocking.

WRAP UP

ACTION ITEMS

List any ideas from this section that can help improve financial results in your beer business.

Write down an action plan: How and when to implement the idea.

Do it now before you forget or get busy with something else. Your income statement is counting on you.

- ☐ ________________________________
- ☐ ________________________________
- ☐ ________________________________
- ☐ ________________________________
- ☐ ________________________________
- ☐ ________________________________
- ☐ ________________________________
- ☐ ________________________________
- ☐ ________________________________
- ☐ ________________________________

SALES GROWTH

INTRODUCTION TO BEER DISTRIBUTOR SALES

THE FIRST LINE ON THE income statement is sales. It's number one on the financial statements and number one in your heart for a good reason: without sales and sales growth, you're out of business.

Sales, revenue, or the top line are different ways of saying the same thing. This is the amount of product sold to the retailer.

A sale occurs when you deliver the beer and the customer signs the invoice. Sales orders or promises to deliver are not sales.

In financial accounting terms, the sale is complete only when the beer is delivered, the retailer takes possession and the invoice is signed. Only then can the admin team book the sale.

These days, sales growth is tough to come by. We face stiff competition from wine, spirits and cannabis (not to mention the thousands of new beer brands). This requires the beer wholesaler to find new tools to increase revenue.

One such tool is finance. Finance isn't just for measuring and keeping score; it can act as a lever to boost sales up. Finance knowledge can help you identify sales growth opportunities and amplify the results.

In this chapter we'll review how to use financial knowledge to build a robust sales growth plan. We'll cover the three primary ways to boost the top line and re-introduce an old-school idea to increase sales: the Tel-Sell Program. Yes, the telephone. People still use it, and it still works to grow sales.

Sharpen your financial pencil, and get ready to grow your beer sales. Sales competition is a battle, and finance is your secret weapon.

HOW TO BUILD A PLAN TO GROW SALES

"Setting goals is the first step in turning the invisible into the visible."

- Tony Robbins

WHAT'S MORE IMPORTANT THAN GROWING sales in your beer business? Not much. So, in this hyper-competitive market, how do you put your company in the best position to increase sales? For starters, you create an amazing sales growth plan.

The sales plan is the road map to grow revenue. It lays out the objectives needed to reach your sales goals. It is a tool that your employees can and should use every day to grow sales.

Below are steps to create an amazing sales growth plan.

1. Get the right people involved
2. Get the right information together
3. Insist on 100% participation and effort
4. Educate your team on the goal of the sales plan

5. Create a sales growth plan for today and update it regularly
6. Share the plan with those who can make it a reality

GET THE RIGHT PEOPLE INVOLVED

The sales manager, inventory manager and financial person should create the sales plan together. They should be in the same room at the same time looking at the same information.

This is a great opportunity to understand how each person, and each department, impacts one another. Inventory management works best with input from sales. Finance works best with input from all departments and can help guide the sales plan process with fancy spreadsheets and historical information.

As a bonus, include an operations person (someone from the warehouse or delivery) in the planning. Delivery and warehouse managers often know a lot about opportunities to grow sales. Tap this resource if you can.

Moreover, there will be product changes in the new year, such as new suppliers, brands and SKUs. Your operations people need to know about this so they can adjust warehouse organization accordingly, and your delivery team needs to know about changes and where to put the beer at retail.

Get the aforementioned three to five people involved in building the plan to grow sales. Each brings different skills to the table, and combined, they are like the Super Friends of sales growth.

GET THE RIGHT INFORMATION TO CREATE THE BEST PLAN

Use historical sales information -- what happened last month, last quarter and last year -- as a starting point to create the new growth plan. Adjust this info based on changes coming in the new year. New suppliers, breweries, and brands will impact the plan. New initiatives, new employees, or new focus will change the plan. Get all this information on paper and baked into your forecast.

Use a template sales tool to fill in the numbers and details. Start simple and get more complicated if it adds value to the process and end result.

Sales Forecast Template						
Annual Sales Forecast						
Measured in $						
	Full Year 2018	Full Year 2018 Growth %	2019 Forecasted Growth	2019 Projected Volume		Notes / Assumptions
Supplier 1	$10,000,000	2.0%	2.0%	$10,200,000		New supplier reps in market
Supplier 2	$1,500,000	5.0%	5.0%	$1,575,000		Adding brand manager
Supplier 3	$450,000	3.5%	0.0%	$450,000		New package design
Supplier 4	$300,000	0.0%	4.0%	$312,000		Introduction of new brands
Supplier 5	$150,000	4.2%	5.0%	$157,500		Now authorized product in large chains
Etc...						
Total	$12,400,000			$12,694,500		

INSIST ON 100% EFFORT AND PARTICIPATION

The biggest issue I've faced when building a growth plan is getting the key people in the same room at the same time. The sales guy always has to deliver a keg or an umbrella somewhere. The inventory manager always has an order to place, and the finance person is busy crunching numbers.

To create a sales growth plan, you need 100% focus, effort and participation from your sales, inventory and finance team. It's a simple rule, but simply doesn't happen that often. The magic of the plan creation is getting together these department heads to communicate and create a sales plan that will work and will kick-butt. Insist on 100% focus on the sales plan.

EDUCATE YOUR TEAM ON THE PURPOSE OF THE SALES PLAN

Sales plans and budgets have a bad reputation. They can be time-consuming, confusing, and pointless, if done wrong. Worst of all, the plan ends up buried in a desk drawer somewhere.

To create a great sales plan, you'll need to educate your team on its purpose, which is, of course, to grow sales and show the team how they can make a difference in achieving this important goal.

Preach to your team that the sales plan is your game plan to grow. It is a road map for the whole organization – sales, operations, admin, everyone. It will be useful every day and provide clarity for all members of your organization.

The sales plan includes what is most important to your beer business -- where you will grow (which retail accounts), how much you'll grow (percentage wise), and who will help get you there. Once your team understands this, they'll understand why it's so important to create a great sales plan.

CREATE A SALES FORECAST NOW AND UPDATE REGULARLY

There's no time like the present to create a kick-butt sales plan. You don't need to wait until the end of the year or end of the quarter - do it now.

In a perfect world, the sales plan is created toward the end of the year and rolled out at the beginning of the new year. This way, the sales team knows their goals and can hit the ground running.

Unfortunately, no one lives in a perfect world.

Things happen and the plan doesn't get done on time. Or the plan does get done, but then the market changes. That 5% growth you projected is looking more like 1%. Now what?

The sales plan should be changed when circumstances change. It should be a flexible, living document that adjusts to the times. Aim to create it in December for the new year, but adjust the plan by March of the new year if it isn't working.

TELL THE WORLD OF YOUR PLAN

If you want to hit your sales plan goals, you need to share it with those who can make a difference. To start, educate your team on how the plan will be achieved. Show them how they fit in and how they can contribute. People like to feel they make a difference in their work, in other words, in your beer business. Give them the direction, vision and leadership and prepare to be amazed.

WRAP UP + ACTION ITEMS

Download the Sales Growth Plan template. Read the notes, input your numbers, and make it your own. Afterward, follow the steps above to create your sales plan. Answer the key questions: Who should be involved, what information is needed, why is this important, and when will the plan be completed. Gather the numbers and rally your team. An amazing sales growth plan is well within your reach.

3 WAYS TO INCREASE DISTRIBUTOR SALES

"Money is plentiful for those who understand the simple laws which govern its acquisition."

- George Clayson

IN AN ERA OF FLAT to declining sales, what can beer distributors do to increase sales? After all, store shelves aren't getting any bigger and customers aren't drinking more beer. Time to put on the thinking cap, get creative and explore new ways to increase the top line sales volume.

In this section, we'll review three ways to increase sales and how each can be applied to your beer business. Business experts have shown that there are only three ways to increase sales. Seems like there should be a million ways to do this, but they fall into just three categories:

1. Increase the number of customers
2. Increase rate of sale (how much retailers spend when they buy)
3. Increase the frequency of sales (how often retailers buy)

Let's dig in and find out how to apply each one to increase beer sales in your business.

INCREASE THE NUMBER OF CUSTOMERS

The typical approach to increase customers is to identify accounts in your market that don't buy from you and try to sell them beer. Distributors run buy/no-buy reports, develop a targeted list of accounts that aren't currently buying, and work to get the sale.

Another approach is to take on a new product line, such as non-alcohol products or snacks. This will allow you to expand distribution to a new account base - usually unlicensed accounts - those accounts that don't sell beer, but do sell non-alcohol drinks and snacks.

There may be opportunities coming soon with cannabis, but that's a story for another day.

If you have the opportunity to buy another beer or non-alcohol beverage distributor in an adjacent market, this will immediately increase the number of customers. With the purchase of the new company, you'll acquire a new market full of new retailers to sell to.

In our business, we have used each of these methods to increase the number of customers. Some are easier or less expensive than others, but all of them increase sales.

INCREASE THE RATE OF SALE

The rate of sale is how much your customers spend when they buy from you. This is determined by running a report of average sales per delivery.

Regular customers tend to buy the same amount of beer every week. There are swings depending on the season or occasion - 4th of July week is crazy busy and the middle of February is slow, for example. Taking out the highs and lows, you'll find that customers have a routine and buy about the same amount every time.

One effective method to increase the rate of sale is to disrupt the routine with the upsell. This is a sales technique wherein the seller suggests additional purchases (upgrades or add-ons) that the customer may like. Amazon is brilliant at upselling customers: "Customers who bought this item also bought these items."

Think about how you can apply the upsell your beer business: "Customers who bought Dogfish 60 Minute IPA also bought Ithaca Flower Power." You get the idea.

Your current customers are your best customers. They know, like, and trust you and they are likely to buy more from you if you suggest products that will help grow their business. The upsell is a great way to increase the rate of sale.

Another idea to increase the rate of sale is to utilize e-commerce in your business. Consider an online list of your beer brands with descriptions, ratings, and glamorous pictures.

Think about it this way: The beer sales person is responsible for selling hundreds of different SKUs. They can't possibly pitch all the products to the retailer during a sales call. However, if the retailer has the option to browse your products online, they may find more of what they need for their business.

If you have a large portfolio of beer products, the e-commerce option may be a good one to increase the rate of sale. Retailers can search your portfolio at their leisure and in their own time. They don't need to be rushed during a 15-minute sales call.

INCREASE THE FREQUENCY OF SALES

The frequency of sales refers to how often your customers buy from you. A typical distributor delivers once a week to smaller accounts and multiple times per week to larger retailers. Here again, there is a routine to the buying activity: The account places the order on a Tuesday and gets the delivery on a Wednesday. Wash, rinse, repeat.

To increase the frequency of sales, look for ways to give your customers additional buying opportunities. For one, email marketing is a great way to announce new products, special offers, or seasonal sales. Retailers won't buy if they don't know the buying opportunity is out there. Two, tell customers about overstocks or discounted items. This gives you another opportunity to increase the frequency of customer purchases.

Another idea is to send targeted offers after a birthday or retailer anniversary. "Happy anniversary - we are celebrating ten years of business together." Everyone loves an anniversary present, especially if it comes with a deal or new product reminder.

WRAP UP + ACTION ITEMS

Retail store shelves aren't expanding and customers aren't buying more beer these days. It's time for you and your team to think outside the box and explore new ways to increase beer sales. As business experts have shown us, there are three basic ways to increase sales:

1. Increase the number of customers. Add a new product line like snacks or non-alcohol brands.
2. Increase rate of sale. Train your sales team to upsell. Think about adding an e-commerce solution - your retailers can shop your brands at their leisure, in their own time, and in their PJs.
3. Increase the frequency of sales. Use email marketing to communicate new products, specials, and even wish a retailer a happy anniversary. Retailers won't buy more frequently unless they know there is a buying opportunity out there. Tell them.

Use these ideas to think about how you can increase sales in your beer business. While there are three main ways to increase sales, there's no limit to creativity and good ideas to accomplish the task. Now, get out there and grow that top line revenue.

HOW TO SELL MORE WITH A TEL SELL PROGRAM

"American business has just forgotten the importance of selling."

- Barry Goldwater

TEL-SELL, OR TELEPHONE SALES, CAN be a great way to increase not only sales but also selling efficiency in your distributorship. Simply put, tel-sell is a selling method wherein the customer order is placed over the phone (or via email or online ordering). This saves time and travel for the route sales team by eliminating or reducing the need to physically call on the account.

There are several considerations with a tel-sell program: choosing the right accounts, training the new staff, and providing excellent customer service. If done poorly, a tel-sell program will cost you customers. If done right, it can increase sales and selling efficiency. Let's focus on how to do it right.

In this section, we'll review a tel-sell process you can implement in your wholesaler business. It works best when you have a formal, structured, and well-thought-out selling plan. To create this plan, follow the Tel-Sell Best Practices.

- The economics of tel-sell
- Provide a high(er) level of service
- Identify tel-sell accounts using 80/20 analysis
- Keep a personal touch

THE ECONOMICS OF TEL-SELL

Not all customers are created equal. Many accounts you sell to are financial losers. The cost to sell, deliver, and service these accounts far exceeds the gross profit on the sale.

Tel-sell provides an opportunity to reduce the costs of servicing these accounts so that you can be profitable. For example, an in-house tel-sell person might make $40k in salary and benefits and will call on 30 accounts a day. An outside sales rep makes $80k and can visit 15 accounts per day. Tel-sell provides an opportunity for twice the number of sales calls at half the cost. Now, that is efficient selling.

Further, tel-sell accounts are generally lower sales volume outlets. By shifting these low volume sales calls in-house, this frees up time for the route sales rep to spend more time at higher volume customers. It's a win-win.

PROVIDE A HIGH LEVEL OF SERVICE

Some distributors shy away from tel-sell, concerned that it will provide a lower level of service to the customer. The worry goes like this: If a sales person doesn't call on the account, it will be impossible to identify and correct problems. Further, without a physical presence in the account, there's no way to build a relationship with the customer, which would lead to increased sales.

These are valid concerns.

The key to a successful tel-sell program is to provide a continued high level of service to the customer. In many cases, a tel-sell program can provide an even higher level of service, with more time attention and follow up for the account.

Think about it this way: A typical route sales person may call on 15 or 20 accounts per day. With travel, delays, and all the small tasks that need to be done, how much time do they really get to sell?

A dedicated tel-sell person has no such distractions. They set up a sales call schedule convenient for the customer. There's plenty of time for the customer to ask questions and the tel-sell rep to provide answers.

An in-house tel sell person is also better positioned to provide information to the retailer on the spot. While in front of a computer, the tel-sell rep can send needed reports or sales materials and quickly answer any questions.

Overall, tel sell can be a much more effective selling process for you and your customer.

IDENTIFY TEL-SELL ACCOUNTS: USE 80/20 ANALYSIS

The process to select tel-sell accounts is a mixture of art and science. An 80/20 analysis provides a good starting point to identify candidates. To get started, run a customer sales report for the last 12 months, sort it from high to low, and analyze the bottom 20 percent of accounts.

From this list, review which ones are new accounts, seasonals or up-and-comers, i.e., those accounts that have the potential to sell more if given more in-person attention.

To help identify good tel-sell account candidates, ask questions like: Are there customers who never have time to see a sales rep? Are there accounts that have asked about online sales or e-commerce options?

Use the numbers and your common sense when selecting accounts for tel-sell. You may be surprised that some accounts would prefer to be on tel-sell. In this case, give them what they want.

KEEP A PERSONAL TOUCH

A tel-sell program should include regular visits to the account owner. This provides an opportunity for the tel-sell person to see the retail location, meet the owner or decision-maker in person, and continue to build the relationship.

The meetings should be set on a schedule and frequency that works for you and the customer – monthly, quarterly, annually, etc. Think of this like a meeting with your banker, insurance broker, or key vendor – you don't need to see these guys all the time, but a face-to-face check once or twice a year is good for everyone.

WRAP UP + ACTION ITEMS

A tel-sell program is a great way to increase sales and selling efficiency in your business. If done properly, this method can save time and resources for your sales team, while continuing to provide a high level of service to your customers.

Run the numbers in your business – the cost of route sales vs. in-house sales – to determine if the tel-sell economics make sense for your business. Analyze your account base for potential candidates, and remember to maintain a personal touch.

Tel-sell can provide a win-win in your distribution business through higher sales, lower costs, and happier customers.

TEL SELL BEST PRACTICES

"The best practice is to follow the advice posted on every railroad crossing: Stop, look and listen."

- Sam Keen

IN THE PREVIOUS SECTION, WE looked at how to use a tel-sell program to increase sales and selling efficiency in your distribution business. Next, we'll dig into tel-sell best practices - the specific steps to make yours successful.

Many distributors have a tel-sell program to solicit orders from smaller, lower volume accounts. This saves time and expense for the route sales team who can then use their time more effectively in larger, higher volume stores.

Shifting the smaller, lower volume accounts to tel-sell does not mean that sales to these outlets have to suffer. The goal is just the opposite: Grow sales and provide as good or better service compared to the route sales person.

Use these best practices to set up a tel-sell program in your beer business:

- Tel-sell training: Accounts, products, and selling techniques
- Tel-sell tools + creative marketing
- Use thank you's to increase sales
- Tel-sell best practices checklist

TEL-SELL TRAINING

"The purpose of training is to tighten up the slack, toughen the body, and polish the spirit."

- Morihei Ueshiba

Training your tel-sell team on products, customers, and selling techniques is key to creating an in-house selling machine. If you already have an excellent sales training program for your route sales team, use it. No need to re-invent the wheel; just be sure to give your tel-sell person the same time, energy, and effort in the training process.

Product training involves learning the portfolio and understanding which brands fit in which retail accounts. Sell sheets on brand attributes and sampling of products are necessary tools in the product training toolkit.

Customer training includes learning about the retail accounts - on/off premise, market type, and ordering history. Learn the specific needs of the account and whether there are special instructions. Training also involves gathering information from the route sales rep who previously sold the account. Moreover, it includes a few road trips. Do the homework, visit the account, and meet in person.

Understand their business better and learn how to serve them better.

Basic training on sales helps your tel-sell person learn how to sell. One tried and true approach is to provide a sales script and conduct role-playing scenarios so the tel-sell person gets to practice their technique freely.

Lastly, don't forget the basics. Provide training on the regular tel-sell sales call schedule and customer delivery day. Understand the day and time when the sales call will be made and the day and time of the customer delivery.

TEL-SELL TOOLS + CREATIVE MARKETING

To make the most of a tel-sell program, a few tools are needed: route accounting software, customer relationship management software and online marketing programs.

- Route accounting software: It has tons of information to help in the sales process. Give your tel-sell person access and teach them how to use it. Access to basic sales reports, delivery schedules, and inventory on-hand are essential for tel-sell.
- Customer relationship management software: Also known as CRM, it gives your tel-sell person an organized snapshot of customers and prospects. With this tool, you can keep track of sales calls, customer notes, and customer satisfaction. Examples include Lillypad or Salesforce.
- Marketing and e-commerce programs: Email marketing is a good way to let customers about new products you're offering.

In addition, it's a great way to share your full product portfolio. A route sales person rarely has time to present more than a handful of brands during a sales call. Email gives your tel sell person the opportunity to share everything you have to offer. Programs like MailChimp or Aweber make it easy to schedule regular marketing emails.

The goal of a tel-sell program is to sell as much or more than with the traditional route sales model. To achieve this, give your customer the ability to make "frictionless purchases." Make it easy for customers to buy from you by letting them place orders via email or your website.

USING THANK YOU TO INCREASE SALES

A simple "thank you" can translate into more sales. Have your tel-sell person go beyond the nuts and bolts of the sales transaction and show regular appreciation to the customer. A 'thank you' can come in many shapes and forms:

- Send your customer a card. Acknowledge a birthday or anniversary, or just send a note of thanks.
- Praise them on social media. Your customer has customers too. Let the world know they provide great service (and great products - yours!)
- Refer business to your customer (and let your customer know).

Lastly, small, thoughtful gifts can go a long way. Give the account something small but meaningful. Everyone loves hats and T-shirts.

WRAP UP + ACTION ITEMS

The goal of a tel-sell program is to grow sales and provide the same or better customer service as the route sales person. It works well when drumming up orders from smaller, lower volume accounts. This saves time and expense for the route sales team who can then use their time more effectively in larger, higher volume stores.

Sales growth and selling efficiency awaits. Put in place a tel-sell program in your beer business today.

WRAP UP

ACTION ITEMS

List any ideas from this section that can help improve financial results in your beer business.

Write down an action plan: How and when to implement the idea.

Do it now before you forget or get busy with something else. Your income statement is counting on you.

☐ ______________________________

☐ ______________________________

☐ ______________________________

☐ ______________________________

☐ ______________________________

☐ ______________________________

☐ ______________________________

☐ ______________________________

☐ ______________________________

☐ ______________________________

GROSS PROFIT

INTRODUCTION TO GROSS PROFIT

FULL DISCLOSURE: I LOVE GROSS profit. Sales are the top priority for beer distributors, but gross profit deserves the same amount of focus.

Think about it this way: A $1 increase in sales will get you 25 cents in gross profit. That 25 cents might make it all the way down to net profit (the bottom line), but probably not.

However, a $1 increase in gross profit is much more likely to get a direct $1 increase in net profit. The idea is to use finance as leverage to improve the bottom line.

To grow sales, you have to spend money. At a certain point, you need more investment in sales personnel, merchandising, and delivery to get that extra dollar of sales. And to increase gross profit, you simply have to spend a little time and ask a few basic questions of your numbers. Indeed, there are many opportunities to increase gross profit. All you have to do is look.

In this chapter, we'll point you in the right direction and present tactics to boost gross profit in your beer business.

Gross profit, the difference between sales and the cost of sales, represents the dollars available to cover all your operating expenses. The cost of sales includes freight, tax, and the beer itself. It also includes the costs related to a bottle bill (if applicable in your state), any duties from imports, and the wholesaler share of discounts or price promotions.

In short, gross profit is a very important number on the income statement. In fact, it might be the most important of them all.

Keep in mind the income statement measures gross profit in two ways: dollars and as a percentage of sales (gross profit $ divided by sales = gross profit percentage).

The gross profit percentage is useful as a benchmark to compare against budget, past performance and industry averages. A typical distributor might have a 25% gross profit goal. This one number is easy to remember and communicate to your employees who can improve the result.

A first step to improve gross profit is to understand what it is and how it's calculated. Next, set a goal for where you need the number to be and engage your team to help improve the number.

In this chapter we'll provide tools and strategies to improve gross profits in your beer business. Sales growth along with gross profit improvement are like love and marriage; they go hand in hand. Read on to learn how to focus on gross profit and improve financial results so that your income statement can live happily ever after.

THE BEST WAY TO IMPROVE PROFITS

THE SINGLE BEST WAY TO increase profits and put more cash in your bank account is to focus on improving your gross profit. Increasing sales may require adding personnel, trucks, and warehouse space. Increasing gross profit requires only your time, attention, and a better process.

REAL MONEY AT STAKE: THE IMPORTANCE OF GP

If you are not focused on gross profit, you are leaving real money on the table. A small fraction of a percentage increase in GP can have a massive impact on your profitability. Many beer distributors focus entirely on sales growth, but I recommend you turn your attention to gross profit.

A few examples: On $25 million of beer sales, a small 0.5% margin improvement equals $125,000 right to the bottom line. On $50 million of sales, this 0.5% increase equals $250,000.

That is some big-time scratch. Best of all, you don't need to add personnel or equipment; you just need to have a better process to funnel these gross profit dollars back into your pocket.

OUR GROSS PROFIT IMPROVEMENT STORY

Sales were growing, but gross profit was shrinking. Something was going wrong with our pricing, discounting, or product costing. We needed to figure out where the problem was and fast. The bottom line depended on it.

At the time, the term gross profit was a mystery to most of our sales people. They had heard about it, but didn't know what it was or why it was important.

Few people understood the gross profit calculation, let alone how to improve it. The sales team was focused only on increasing sales. The inventory team was focused on making sure we had enough inventory (but not too much). The two teams would talk to each other, but not really. Their agendas were different and so were their incentives.

The first step was to show our team how gross profit worked and how they could work together to increase it. The process was an eye-opener for everyone involved. We started by teaching the basics.

GROSS PROFIT BASICS

Before you can improve gross profit, everyone involved needs to know how it is calculated. The math isn't hard. It's just sales minus the cost of goods. For example, if you sell a case of beer for $32 and the cost is $22, you have a $10 gross profit.

Next, you can think of that $10 gross profit as a percentage by dividing it by sales. This makes the number easy to compare to a planned outcome. For example, if the budget calls for a 25% gross profit on all sales, you can see where you stand compared to the goal. Continuing the example above, $10 gross profit divided by $32 sales equals a 31.25% GP percentage.

To avoid confusion, be consistent with the costs included in your gross profit calculation. For example, some distributors include handling fees for bottle deposits in their product costs. Other distributors include mandatory marketing expenses.

Regardless of what costs you include or exclude, the most important thing is to be consistent. Otherwise, your gross profit calculations will superficially fluctuate and make it difficult to compare current results to past performance. When you understand the different pieces of the gross profit puzzle and how they work, you can improve the number.

OUR PROCESS: A SINGULAR FOCUS ON INCREASING GROSS PROFIT

Once our team knew why gross profit was vital to company success and understood how it worked, the next step was to put this knowledge into action to improve the number.

We set up regular gross profit meetings with our GM, sales manager, and inventory manager. The purpose was to get everyone working towards the same goal of increasing gross profit.

The meeting agenda was the same each week:

- Review the actual gross profit compared to the plan – what was the income statement telling us?

- Run profit analysis reports by supplier to identify under-performing brands
- Isolate the components of gross profit and determine where we could improve

What we found during the first meetings was that the sales and inventory teams were not communicating at all. Operating separately, they only focused on their individual agenda.

The sales manager would meet with the supplier, negotiate pricing, and a discounting schedule. The inventory manager would place product orders according to expected market demand. No one, however, was looking at the gross profit calculation.

In many cases, it turned out that the pricing during discount periods was so low that it killed the gross profit for the whole year. After this was discovered, the sales and inventory manager worked with the suppliers and negotiated better depletion allowance support.

In other cases, an average freight cost was used to compute the product costs. Upon closer inspection, the sales and inventory manager determined that the actual freight cost was significantly higher than the estimated freight charge given by the supplier.

The process of getting sales and inventory on the same page and working towards the same goal helped us significantly increase our gross profit.

USE TECHNOLOGY TO SUPERCHARGE YOUR PROCESS

After identifying and correcting the big problems dragging down our gross profit, our next move was to drill deeper to find more ways to improve the number.

We ran multiple profit analysis reports through our route accounting system. We looked at GP by brand and by SKU, by class of trade (chain grocery, convenience, etc.), and by individual customer. The goal was to identify areas where gross profit was low and figure out ways to increase it. This approach was not rocket science, but it worked to improve our gross profit and our bottom line.

WRAP UP + ACTION ITEMS

As beer distributors, we love sales growth. However, the most efficient way to increase profits and put more cash in your bank account is to focus on improving gross profit. A small improvement in the gross profit percentage can add up to big money fast.

- Teach your employees the gross profit basics
- Set up regular GP review meetings with a singular focus on improving gross profit

Implement the steps above and let the results surprise you.

THREE STEPS TO IMPROVE GROSS PROFIT

> *"The trouble with the profit system has always been that it was highly unprofitable to most people."*
>
> \- *E.B. White*

EVERY NUMBER ON YOUR INCOME statement is important, but few are as critical as gross profit. The sales line measures how much product we sell to the retailer, but gross profit measures how much distributors get to keep to cover operating costs. About 75% of sales dollars go straight to the supplier, freight carrier and tax man. On $100,000 of sales, $75,000 is already spent. In other words, sales are for the supplier, but gross profit is for the distributor.

In this section we will review a 3-step process to improve gross profit and grow the bottom line:

1. Know your gross profit (GP). Understand how the calculation works and the components of GP.
2. Build a team and process to focus on increasing gross profit.

3. Love your GP. Give it extra time and attention. Sales are critical, but gross profit needs your love just as much. Remember, this is the only portion of the sales dollar you get to keep. It's up to you to make the most of it.

KNOW YOUR GP: UNDERSTAND HOW TO CALCULATE GROSS PROFIT

The basic equation is sales minus cost of goods equals gross profit. Sales show up first on the income statement, followed by the cost of sales. More specifically, the sale is the amount on the customer invoice. When the product is delivered and signed for, accounting magic happens and turns the transaction into a sale. The sum of all the customer deliveries makes its way into the sales line on the income statement.

The cost of sales typically includes three things: cost of the product, freight cost to get the product to your warehouse and the alcohol taxes due on the sale. The route accounting system tracks the costs associated with each product in your inventory records. This cost is then calculated on every sale, and rolled up into the cost of sales on the income statement.

Gross profit is shown on the income statement in dollars and as a percentage of sales. Looking at GP as a percentage makes it easier to determine if you're on track with your profit plan. Make sure you and your team all the aspects discussed in this section.

BUILD A TEAM TO IMPROVE YOUR GP

Once you understand the math behind the GP, you have the power to improve the number. But you can't do it alone; you'll need some help from your team: 1) Get buy-in from ownership: GP is #1; 2) Create the GP Review Process: The road map to GP improvement; and 3) Establish the GP team: Leverage the collective wisdom of the team.

1. SET THE TONE FROM THE TOP: GP IS #1

For many distributors, GP is not #1 on the priority list. It's not even number 2, 3, or 4. It usually falls somewhere after sales growth, out of stocks, and out of code inventory.

The first step is setting the tone within your organization that improving gross profit is a key success factor. Ownership and upper management need to wave the flag of GP, or the troops won't get behind it. This sounds easy enough, but it won't be if your company has always focused exclusively on sales growth.

The tone from the top has to be that gross profit is a priority, and everyone on the GP team will be expected to plan, prepare, and participate in the meetings. This will make it easier to get buy-in from the sales team members who would rather be anywhere than in a gross profit review meeting.

2. CREATE A PROCESS TO REVIEW GP

The process to review gross profit can take many forms, but I've found it helpful to start with a look at the top line metrics. Keep things simple and focus on the numbers that matter most.

The gross profit scorecard shows the total company GP % goal compared to actual results. It provides a starting point to discuss how the company goal was created – for example, use of historical trends, changes to product mix, etc. And it gives an opportunity to question and discuss the goal. At regular intervals, take a step back to make sure everyone understands how GP is calculated.

After the top line numbers are reviewed, discussed, and understood, it's time to dig into the details of gross profit. Below are examples of reports to monitor and analyze GP results:

- GP by product line vs. goal (beer, wine, non-alcohol if you have them)
- GP by supplier – actuals vs. expectations
- GP by supplier, brand, and item
- GP by chain/independent
- GP by account

You can go as deep as you need to, but ease into it. It's tempting to get lost in the details and start chasing a minor issue. Keep it top line to start and go after the big dollars.

Below are common issues to be wary of during the GP review:

- Is the pricing correct? Your sales or pricing coordinator usually has this stuff memorized. Are there any obvious errors (for example, pricing changes that didn't get inputted into the system).
- Are the costs correct? Your inventory person knows the cost components: FOB/product, freight, taxes. Is it complete and accurate?
- Are all the depletion allowances/supplier billbacks properly accounted for? I've seen this before where one person cuts a deal with a supplier to bill something back, but they don't tell the person who actually inputs the deal in the system. All of a sudden, you have a 10% GP when you should have 25%.

3. ESTABLISH THE GP TEAM

Depending on the size of your company, the GP team should include at least one person from sales, inventory management, finance, and operations. Each person brings a different expertise and perspective to the work at hand.

Generally speaking, the sales guy wants to discount everything to increase sales – gross profit be damned. The finance guy doesn't want to sell anything unless it meets or exceeds the gross profit goals. The inventory and operations people just want to know which numbers to put in the system.

Despite these differences, it is the diversity of expertise and perspective that will get you a great result. It won't always be easy, but opening up communication, educating the team, and focusing on a common goal will be a win for your gross profit.

In our company, we had the following people on the GP Team:

- Finance/CFO: lead the team, ensure everyone understands the numbers
- Inventory manager: review product costs for completeness and accuracy
- Sales manager/Pricing coordinator: review pricing, discounting, for accuracy
- Operations/GM: implement delivery, warehouse or operational changes needed to achieve GP goals

First and foremost, the GP Team exists to monitor, manage, and improve gross profit. Despite the obvious differences in roles, responsibilities and agendas, the team must focus on a single mission: to improve gross profit.

The team should meet on a regular basis and follow the GP process as established above. Below are GP meeting best practices:

- Meeting basics: Nobody likes long, drawn-out, pointless meetings. So, don't have those. Instead, begin and end on time, send an agenda well in advance, and meet to make decisions and take action.
- Take meeting notes and distribute to the team. Write it down or it didn't happen.
- Plan and prepare in advance of the meeting. Run reports that need to be run, review them, come prepared with insights and action items to share.

LOVE YOUR GP

The sales line gets a lot of attention, but gross profit needs your love just as much. This is the only portion of the sales dollar that distributors get to keep, so it's up to you to make the most of it. Give your gross profit the time and attention it deserves, and you will see the benefit on your bottom line.

Every number on the income statement is important, but few numbers are as key as your GP. Sales are for the supplier, and gross profit is for you, the distributor. Implement the three steps outlined above to start improving your GP today.

COMMON ERRORS IN GROSS PROFIT... AND HOW TO FIX THEM

"Variability has the potential to create confusion."

- Steven Redhead

A DISTRIBUTOR FRIEND CALLED ME recently with a concern about his gross profit. He was seeing a lot of fluctuation in monthly gross profit percentage. Some months it was too low (20%), while other months it was too high (30%). My friend asked what the cause might be and how he could fix it.

Variation in monthly gross profit can cause confusion, uncertainty, and a lack of faith in the accuracy of the numbers. More importantly, it may be a symptom of a big problem in your financial system that needs to be fixed.

In this section, I will share the same action steps I gave my friend to solve his gross profit problem.

3 CAUSES OF ERRORS IN MONTHLY DISTRIBUTOR GROSS PROFIT

1. Inventory received, but the purchase expense not recorded
2. Inventory value does not match actual costs
3. Empty barrels and pallets are returned, but credit not recorded

CAUSE #1: INVENTORY RECEIVED, BUT PURCHASE EXPENSE NOT RECORDED

Very often, inventory is received into the warehouse, but the related invoice has not arrived. The accounting transaction records the value of the inventory, but the purchase expense isn't recorded. In this case, gross profit for the month will be overstated.

This can happen at any time throughout the month, but it causes the biggest variance when it occurs at the end. For example, the inventory is received and recorded in January, but the invoice and purchase expense is recorded in February. In this circumstance, the gross profit will be overstated for January and understated for February.

Over time, these variations sort themselves out, but when you look at month-to-month gross profit, there are inconsistencies. To determine if you have this problem in your company, do a test of inventory receipts and match them up to your supplier invoices. Test when the inventory receipts and related purchase expenses are recorded. If they do not occur in the same month, your gross profit will be incorrect. Fortunately, this problem is easy to identify and easy to fix.

Many accounting systems have the capability to create an open purchase order report. It shows whether inventory was received but not matched up with an invoice. If the invoice doesn't arrive on time, the expense is still recorded. The asset received (inventory) is matched up in the same month with the related expense (purchase).

To check for this potential problem in your business, have your finance team test the idea above to make sure you are properly matching up the inventory receipt with the related purchase expense.

CAUSE #2: INVENTORY VALUE DIFFERS FROM ACTUAL COSTS

Inventory can be valued in a number of different ways. One such valuation method is to use standard costs. A standard cost involves using the expected FOB and freight costs for the products.

The potential problem with using standard costs is that costs change. A supplier may increase its price, or the freight cost to get product to your warehouse may go up significantly. Recall when gas prices went through the roof and every freight carrier was charging excessive surcharges.

When actual costs change, and standard costs are not updated, you will get variations in monthly gross profit percentages.

To see if you have this problem in your distribution business, have your finance person test your actual costs compared to your standard product costs.

Start with your top five or ten selling SKUs and pull the related supplier invoices. Check the inventory value of the product (the FOB and freight) and compare it to the most recent supplier invoice. If there are differences, it may be time to adjust the standard cost of your inventory. This process ensures your inventory value matches the purchase expense, and it will smooth out fluctuations in monthly gross profit percentage.

CAUSE #3: EMPTY KEGS RETURNED, BUT CREDIT NOT RECORDED

Breweries charge distributors a deposit for kegs and pallets. The value of the deposits, say $30 per keg and $15 per pallet, is recorded in the inventory value. When empty kegs and pallets are returned to the supplier, they are deducted from inventory and a credit will be due to the distributor.

Fluctuations in gross profit can occur when the kegs/pallets are sent back (and value deducted from inventory), but the corresponding credit due back from the brewery is not recorded. This can happen at any time during the month, but usually occurs at month end.

Check for this problem your system. Have your finance team test the timing of when kegs/pallets are removed from inventory and when the credit from the brewery is recorded. If the deduction occurs in one month and the credit occurs in another, you'll have a variance in gross profit.

WRAP UP + ACTION ITEMS

Monthly gross profit variances cause frustration and confusion for owners and managers in your beer business. It is hard to have faith in the financial statements when the gross profit changes so much from month to month. More importantly, these fluctuations may be a symptom of a bigger problem in your operations.

To correct variability in your distributor gross profit, test for these common problems:

1. Inventory received, but the purchase expense not recorded
2. Inventory value does not match actual costs
3. Empty barrels and pallets are returned, but credit not recorded

The tests are quick and easy, while the benefits to your company and financial reporting are long-lasting. Fix your gross profit errors and restore confidence in your financial statements.

WRAP UP

ACTION ITEMS

List any ideas from this section that can help improve financial results in your beer business.

Write down an action plan: How and when to implement the idea.

Do it now before you forget or get busy with something else. Your income statement is counting on you.

- ☐ ______________________
- ☐ ______________________
- ☐ ______________________
- ☐ ______________________
- ☐ ______________________
- ☐ ______________________
- ☐ ______________________
- ☐ ______________________
- ☐ ______________________
- ☐ ______________________

OPERATING EXPENSES

INTRODUCTION TO OPERATING EXPENSES

OPERATING EXPENSES ARE THE DAY-TO-DAY costs to run your business. They include all the costs on the income statement that aren't directly related to the cost of goods sold. Operating costs are often referred to as "below the line" expenses - as they are below the gross profit calculation line on the income statement.

Operating expenses include items like payroll, insurance, utilities, and rent. These expenses are then grouped and sub-totaled by department. For example, a beer distributor may have expenses grouped into the following departments:

- Sales
- Merchandising
- Delivery
- Warehouse
- Administration
- Maintenance

In this chapter, we'll review tips and strategies to manage and reduce your beer business's operating expenses. Every dollar saved is an extra dollar to the bottom line -- that's what my grandpa used to say.

What we'll cover:

- The one question technique to reduce expense
- A system to ensure only proper expenses are paid
- Three quick wins: Specific ideas you can implement to reduce expenses right away

No need to wait around to save money. Let's get into the good stuff and show you how to reduce expenses in your beer business.

THE BEST TOOL TO CONTROL SPENDING

"Frugality includes all the other virtues."

- Cicero

THE BEST WAY TO MAKE more money in your beer business is to spend less money. Plain and simple. However, it gets complicated when you try to figure out where, exactly, to cut back.

In this section, we'll kick off a review of operating expenses and how you can reduce them. First, we'll look at the power of purchase orders to help you control spending in your distribution business. This simple tool helps ensure the hard-earned money you spend on supplies, materials and equipment is spent properly.

A purchase order, or a document issued by a buyer (you) to a seller (your vendor), indicates the type, quantity, and price of products or services you want to buy. It is used to control purchases as well as company spending.

How to control spending in your company:

- Approve the spend before making the spend. Too often, it's done the other way around.
- Get the details. What are we buying and why?
- Understand the cash flow. What is the impact of spending on cash flow? How much cash will be needed and when will it be spent?

APPROVE THE SPEND

Most of the time, we buy what is needed, then we figure out the details later. It seems like the right thing to do, but it can cost your beer business a lot of money in unnecessary spending.

First, have someone in your company approve all spending over a certain limit. The limit can be $1 or $5,000, whatever is a material amount for your business. The simple fact that a second person will be reviewing and approving any expenditures will reduce spending.

Human nature is a funny thing. If you know someone is going to double check your work, you will make an effort to make sure you've done it right. The same thing goes for spending money. If you know someone else is going to check your decision to spend money, you'll make sure you're spending it properly.

Have your managers fill out a purchase order for any spending over $500. Let managers know that you will personally review any requested spending over the limit. Also, tell them to do research before the spend and ask some basic questions:

- Do we really need to buy this? What is the business need?

- Can we buy this cheaper somewhere else? What other vendors have you checked with?
- Is there another way to solve this problem without spending cash?

A few questions can save a lot of dollars.

Get the Details: What Are We Buying?

Managers who request to buy things know the details of the purchase. Make sure they write it down on the purchase order, so everyone else knows the details too.

I've seen many purchase orders that do not describe what is being purchased. The form might say, "supplies" or "spare parts" or something equally vague. A lack of details makes it difficult to determine what was purchased (and why).

Insist on a good description to provide a clear picture of what is being purchased and save time on reviewing the purchase order.

Additionally, teach your managers to use general ledger numbers. The heart and soul of the financial statements, these are the categories of where the money is being spent. As general ledger account numbers create the financial statements, give your managers a list of the numbers they need to know. This helps ensure that expenses they incur end up in the right section on the financial statements.

UNDERSTAND THE CASH FLOW

Purchase orders help you understand the cash flow of your beer business.

- What do we plan to spend?
- How much cash do we need and when will we need it?
- How much cash (or borrowing capability) do we have?

By using purchase orders, you will have advance approval of any spending and information to answer each of the questions above.

The first rule of business is "Don't Run Out of Cash." Purchase orders give you visibility of upcoming cash flows so you don't run out.

WRAP UP + ACTION ITEMS

A little form called a purchase order can give you major control over company spending. Insist that your managers provide a good description of WHAT they are buying and WHY Are there alternatives to making the spend? Can the item be bought cheaper elsewhere?

You work hard for every dollar that comes into your distribution business. It only makes sense to ask some tough questions before spending money.

ONE QUESTION TECHNIQUE TO REDUCE COSTS

"There is nothing so useless as doing efficiently that which should not be done at all."

- Peter Drucker

LIKEWISE, THERE IS NOTHING SO painful as spending money that should not be spent at all.

In this section, we'll present a technique that you can use to identify and eliminate spending that doesn't make a real difference in your business. And believe me, you have these un-necessary expenses, just like most other beer distributors.

- The one question technique to identify and reduce unnecessary spending
- The 5 supporting questions to zero in on wasteful spending
- How to put the technique into action

THE ONE QUESTION

Zig Ziglar, an author, salesman, and motivational speaker, wrote and spoke about a number of topics including sales, success, and goal setting. As part of his goal-setting techniques, Ziglar discussed the one question that you should ask to determine whether you are on the right path to achieving your goals. The question was designed to be simple, but powerful: Does this move me closer to or further from my goals?

If the goal is to lose weight, the question could be applied to a variety of decisions throughout the day. Does this cheeseburger move me closer to or further from my goals? Does an extra 30 minutes on the treadmill move me closer to or further from my goals?

In the beer business, we can re-frame the question to help identify and eliminate spending that does not move us towards our goals: Does this expense move our company closer to or further from our goals?

The next time you review a stack of invoices or sign the checks, ask yourself the one question. It might just save you a bundle.

THE 5 SUPPORTING QUESTIONS

The one question technique is useful to identify, in a general sense, whether an expense or group of expenses should exist in your business. The next step is to ask 5 supporting questions to gain a better understanding of your goals and determine whether the expense should be eliminated.

In our business, we identified the 5 supporting questions listed below. They represented our corporate objectives and what was most important for our business. In a sense, these were our company goals:

1. Does this expense make us a better company?
2. Does it improve customer service?
3. Does it improve working conditions, safety, or morale for our employees?
4. Does it improve our community?
5. Does it provide a return on investment?

Customer service, employee morale and safety, support of the community, and return on investment were our primary company goals. We added the more general question - "does this make us better" - as a catch-all for things we couldn't define specifically. Sometimes, a spend doesn't fit neatly into the other goal categories, but you may feel in your gut that it will make you a better company.

HOW TO TAKE ACTION + REDUCE EXPENSES

Let's cover the specific steps to apply the aforementioned technique in your beer business so that you can start saving money.

1. Find out how and where money leaves your business. Cash flows out of your business through accounts payable, payroll, manual checks and EFT or ACH deductions directly from your bank account.
2. Insert yourself into the money-out process. Put yourself directly in between your money and the expense to be paid. In other words, sign every check that goes out through accounts payable, review every manual check before it is mailed, look over the payroll report before it is processed, and get a listing

of all the EFT or ACH payments that have been processed through your bank account.

3. Do one thing at a time + ask the one question. You'll find out that money leaves your beer business in a lot of different ways. Start with just one thing: accounts payable. Before signing the check, take a look at the invoice and apply the one question technique.
4. Review past spending. One of my favorite financial reports is the general ledger (G/L). It records every transaction that flows through your business. Print a copy of your G/L for the prior month to take a look at all the expenses. Do you know what they are? Do they make sense? Ask the one question and the 5 supporting questions.

Follow the steps above to find and eliminate unnecessary expenses in your beer business.

WRAP UP + ACTION ITEMS

The best way to make more money is to stop spending money on things that don't matter. The one question and 5 supporting questions will help you find and eliminate these meaningless drains on your cash flow.

Review the accounts payable and your general ledger. Ask the questions of every spend. If you can't answer yes to any of the questions, it's time to eliminate the expense.

3 SPECIFIC WAYS TO CUT COSTS

NOW THAT YOU HAVE THE background in how to control spending by using purchase orders, let's dig into specific strategies you can implement right away to reduce operating expenses in your beer business. Each strategy will provide you with quick, profitable and proven results.

I have used each of these ideas to make huge reductions in operating expenses. If you follow the steps, I believe you will get similar results in your business.

- How to Reduce Health Insurance Costs (and Empower Your Employees to Share in the Savings)
- How to Pay Less in Property Taxes (How we Saved $20,000 per Year with Only a Few Hours of Work)
- How to Lower Energy Costs (How a Small Change Saved Over $100,000 in Operating Expenses)

Think of these ideas as quick wins. They offer easy ways to save thousands, tens of thousands, or even hundreds of thousands of dollars in your business.

Everybody likes to win. Everybody likes to save money. Let's combine the two and get results for your business.

REDUCE HEALTH INSURANCE EXPENSE

"Nobody likes insurance companies, especially health insurance companies."

- P.J. O'Rourke

HEALTH INSURANCE IS ONE OF the biggest expenses on your income statement. After the cost of purchasing inventory and making payroll, health insurance is usually the third largest expense a beer distributor will have.

According to the Kaiser Foundation, KFF.org, the average premium for an employer-sponsored family health plan has increased 58% in the last 10 years to over $18,000. And it just keeps going up - the historical trend line is 6% to 12% annual increases.

Time to panic.

The financial aspects of the health system in the US are fundamentally flawed. Lack of transparency in pricing makes it nearly impossible for a consumer to know what they are paying for. Traditional hospitals and clinics remain entrenched in the standard ways of doing business with little incentive to change.

Doctors and administrative staff make a lot of money, and any change to the system to operate differently, in a more transparent or competitive manner, is a threat to their livelihood. Beer distributors, like all other employers who provide health insurance, are the victims of this bloated system.

So, other than complaining about it, what can we do to lower health costs?

Here's an idea: Look into a self-funded health plan. We used a self-funded plan for well over a decade and saved millions of dollars.

No joke. Compared to a traditional, fully funded health plan like Anthem Blue Cross or United Health Care, our company's self-funded plan continually saved us between 30% to 70% on health care costs every year.

In doing the research for this section, I was surprised to learn that 63% of workers are covered by a self-funded health plan. Everybody's doing it, and maybe you should too.

The first step is to contact a broker to learn about the details of a self-funded plan. What are the risks and rewards? How do you set up a self-funded plan? Are the benefits better or worse than those offered now?

There's plenty to learn, but it's all worth it if you can save half on your health insurance expense. Below I share what I know so that you'll have a basic understanding of how self-funded plans work. I'll also include resources and links to more details.

SELF-INSURED VS. FULLY INSURED PLANS

A myriad of health plan options are out there, but they generally fall into two broad choices for employee health insurance: a self-insured or fully insured commercial plan like Anthem Blue Cross or Harvard Pilgrim.

In a self-insured plan, the employer acts as the insurance company and assumes the financial risk for the health plan costs. Each health claim is paid from dollar one, and re-insurance is used to protect against very large claims that exceed a certain dollar amount. The costs of the plan can vary greatly depending on how much your employees utilize the health care.

With a fully insured plan, the employer pays a fixed premium to the insurance carrier - the amount of the premium doesn't change during the policy period, whether there's one claim or one hundred claims. From a budgeting standpoint, this provides some comfort as you know what your health costs are going to be month to month. However, at renewal time those costs always go up. As noted above, the average cost of a fully insured family plan has increased 58% in the last decade.

RISKS AND REWARDS

"The biggest risk is not taking any risk..."

- Mark Zuckerberg

The prospect of assuming the financial risk for your employee's health costs sounds scary, and it can be. You hear stories all the time about catastrophic medical issues and the extremely high costs to pay for treatment.

With a fully insured plan, you don't foot the bill for any individual claim; you simply pay a fixed premium. If there's one claim or a hundred, the premium stays the same. That is a comforting feeling; however, it's a false comfort. You're guaranteed to pay a set amount, but you're virtually guaranteed to pay too much. Now, that's risky.

To reduce the cost risk, a self-funded plan uses re-insurance to protect against large claims that exceed a certain dollar amount. This way, the plan's cost exposure is capped at a certain level. These caps are known as specific and aggregate deductibles.

A specific deductible is the maximum your plan will pay for any one person during the policy year. An aggregate deductible is the max the plan will pay for the sum of all claims.

This is about the time when your eyes start to glaze over, but just remember that this idea could save you half on your health insurance expense. Look at that health expense line item on your income statement, cut it in half and tell me that isn't a huge savings. Now, that's a big reward.

BASIC COMPONENTS OF A SELF-FUNDED PLAN

A broker can help you design a plan, explain the risks and rewards in greater detail, and determine if a self-insured option is right for your beer business. That said, here is the template that we use in our self-insured plan.

1. Specific and aggregate deductibles cap our out of pocket claims costs
2. Fixed premium amount for re-insurance
3. Fixed fees for third-party administrator costs

Plan Deductibles: Out of pocket costs. Each year we look at our deductibles and determine if it makes sense to increase these numbers or leave them be. Just like the deductible on your car insurance, you can get a lower premium if you raise the number - you assume a bit more risk in exchange for a lower premium. We do the same with our specific and aggregate deductibles. Our broker does the analysis, explains our options, and makes a recommendation.

Re-insurance. Think of re-insurance as insurance for the insurance company. In a self-funded plan, you are the insurance company. Re-insurance gives you the protection against large claims. A separate policy is purchased, and a fixed premium is paid. Again, your broker will do the analysis and solicit competitive bids.

Third party administrator (TPA): These are the people who take care of the nuts and bolts of your plan. They review claims, process paperwork, and pay the bills (with your money). Together, you create a health plan document, the operating manual for your plan, and your TPA makes sure the rules are followed.

Your TPA also provides a wealth of information to you, regarding health care utilization and ways to save money. This gives you the ability to control some of your health plan costs previously out of your control.

RESOURCES

To learn more about the details of self-insured plans, check out the Self-Insurance Institute of America website. Here, you'll find more information about group plans, stop-loss re-insurance, and plan design.

The Self Insurance Educational Foundation is another great resource to learn about the pros and cons risks and rewards of self-insurance.

WRAP UP

Under either option, self-insured or fully insured, health care costs are unpredictable. With a fully insured plan, you have a fixed premium and know exactly what you'll pay. However, you also know that the premium will increase next year, and the next and the next. You'll have the comfort of being able to budget the annual cost, but you'll never know from one year to the next how much more the cost will be.

With a self-insured plan, you will have fixed costs for your re-insurance premium and third-party administrator fees, but the claim costs will be variable. Some months, you may have very few claims; others, you can get whacked pretty hard. The re-insurance will take away most of the risk of a catastrophic claim, but you'll still need to ride the ups and downs of medical claim activity.

We've just scratched the surface here, but this idea is powerful enough to create huge savings for your organization. It might just be powerful enough to save the entire health care system.

Call your broker, take action, and save half on your health care expenses today.

REDUCE HEALTH INSURANCE... EVEN MORE

> *"Competition is the keen cutting edge of business, always shaving away at costs."*
>
> *- Henry Ford*

IF SWITCHING TO A SELF-FUNDED health plan is right for your beer business, you may be able to save a huge pile of money. One way to make that pile of money bigger is to teach your employees to shop for health care services, then give them a piece of the cost savings when they find it.

We live in the greatest country in the world. We have a free market and capitalism abounds. Let's use some of that capitalist spirit to drive down health insurance costs for employees and your beer business.

In this section, we'll review why teaching your employees to shop for health care might be the biggest cost-saving move you can make. When employees shop and save on health care, everyone saves money.

- Health insurance: What it costs, what you can save, what's at stake

- Avoid these health expense savings traps: The usual approach to saving isn't working
- Use the free market: Teach employees to comparison shop and let them share in the savings

HEALTH INSURANCE: WHAT IT COSTS AND WHAT YOU CAN SAVE

According to the Kaiser Foundation, the average cost of a family health plan is $18,000 per year and rising. This is big bucks for a marginal plan with high deductibles and limited provider options for employees.

If you have 100 employees and cover 60% of the cost, this expense adds up to over a million dollars per year. That is a lot of money for a mediocre benefit plan. Fortunately, a self-funded health plan can provide huge savings and superior benefits for your employees.

In my experience with self-funded health insurance, the total cost of a family health plan was $6,000 per year. The deductibles were very low, and the provider network was wide. Compare this to the $18,000 average noted earlier, and you can see how much money this type of plan can save your business.

Health insurance goes up and up because no one in the system has an incentive for it to go down. Doctors, hospitals and other providers are getting paid. It's up to you and your employees to try a new approach so that you can reduce this huge expense in your beer business. With a self-funded plan, you can create a system with built-in incentives to drive down costs for everyone.

AVOID THESE HEALTH EXPENSE SAVINGS TRAPS

Many companies take a soft approach to health care savings. There are reimbursements for gym memberships, free flu shots, and hand sanitizer around every corner. These are all good things and done with the best of intentions for employees. However, they barely scratch the surface when it comes to saving any money on health costs.

Some companies pay employees to leave the health plan. The idea here is that the best way to reduce health costs is to have fewer employees in the plan.

In this scenario, if an employee can be covered on another health plan (like their spouse's plan) they are offered an amount to do so. This is typically a voluntary move that the employee needs to agree to, and they are paid cash as an incentive.

The employer wins because there is one less person in the plan, the employee wins because they pocket some cash. Ideally, the employee will have compared plans, done the math, and determined which health option is best for their family. But usually they don't. They take the cash and run.

This option seems interesting on the surface – I will pay you to go get health care somewhere else. However, this is akin to kicking the can down the road. Nothing is done to fundamentally change the total costs in the system.

TEACH EMPLOYEES TO PRICE SHOP FOR HEALTH CARE

The single best way to reduce health care costs is to teach employees how to price shop for services and let them share in the savings when they find it. When you think about it, this makes a lot of sense. You ask employees to shop and compare prices for everything in your beer business – office supplies, freight charges, warehouse equipment, and so on. Shopping health care costs should be no different, especially when these costs are among the biggest expense items on the income statement.

So, why isn't this done all the time? Why isn't price shopping for health care services a mainstream, generally accepted way of doing business? There are a few reasons.

- Lack of price transparency: There's no value menu for health insurance
- Lower cost health care equals lower quality: Perception vs. reality
- We trust our doctor: Why take a chance on somebody else?
- There's no incentive to shop around for a better deal

1. Lack of price transparency: Hospitals and health care providers don't readily share information about what services cost. There's no menu of prices you can look up online to compare prices and no easy way to figure out whether Hospital A vs. B is over-charging. This lack of price transparency makes it difficult and time-consuming to figure out the best price and the best deal for your money. You can find out, but it takes some effort.

2. Lower cost equals lower quality: We don't want to shop for health care because we fear that it will lead to lower quality care. There is a perception that if something costs less, it might be inferior. No one wants to take a chance on inferior health care.

However, there are many circumstances where a procedure costs less and the quality of care is far better than the more costly provider. We found this to be the case with Boston, Massachusetts area hospitals as compared to our rural hospitals in New Hampshire. The Boston hospitals offer lower prices and superior results for their patients. Why? Competition.

The Boston hospitals employ doctors that perform the same type of surgeries hundreds of times. They are experts. They also compete against other area hospitals for the business. This drives down prices while providing excellent care.

3. We trust our doctor: Why take a chance on somebody else? Consider a circumstance where you need to have knee surgery. Your doctor refers you to a surgeon at the local hospital and talks you through the process. He tells you what to expect and how long the recovery period will be. You trust your doctor and trust his referral. The easy approach is to simply follow your doctor's recommendation. However, your doctor really doesn't care how much the procedure costs or whether it's cheaper somewhere else. Their job is to get you fixed up, not to save money. Saving money is your job.

4. There's no incentive to shop around for a better deal. If you give employees a reason to compare prices, and let them share in the savings, they will find a way to overcome all the resistance points noted above. With an incentive to shop around, employees will figure out how much health care costs at different providers. They will find the lowest price and the best service.

WRAP UP + ACTION ITEMS

Your employees shop for everything – toothpaste, a loaf of bread, a new car. However, they haven't yet been taught how to shop for health insurance.

Thus, this action item is simple: Teach your employees how to shop for health care and give them a piece of the savings when they find it. The power of the free market combined with the employee's incentive to save money will drive down costs for everyone, especially on your income statement.

REDUCE PROPERTY TAXES

"Costs do not exist to be calculated. Costs exist to be reduced."

-- Taiichi Ohno

IT IS REMARKABLE HOW MANY ways our beer business gets taxed. It's like in the movie Forrest Gump when Bubba was talking about shrimp.

"There's shrimp gumbo, pan fried, deep fried, stir fried, pineapple shrimp, lemon shrimp, coconut shrimp..."

Same deal with taxes. We've got federal income taxes, state income taxes, payroll taxes, beer taxes, real property taxes, personal property taxes ... the list is endless.

No one likes paying taxes, so let's review an idea to use an outside service to reduce one of your tax obligations: the dreaded and ever-increasing property tax.

Disclaimer: As we are talking taxes, this is the part where I say, this is not tax advice. The content here is provided for informational purposes only. Make sure to check with your tax professional first to determine if this idea makes sense for your business. Okay, let's continue.

Property tax is calculated by multiplying the tax rate by the assessed value of the property – land and buildings. For beer distributors, this can be a sizable expense due to the value of office space and large warehouses.

Both the property tax rate and the assessed value change on a regular basis. Some years the rate goes up and the assessment goes down. In other years, it's just the opposite – the rate goes down and the assessment goes up. Either way, the one thing that doesn't change is that the total tax bill always goes up.

The process to assess the value of a property is subjective at best. Appraisers use comparable property sales and other metrics to gauge value, but rarely are two properties alike. Therefore, the value assigned to properties is an approximation, an estimate, a best guess. So why not hire your own consultant to make a better estimate?

OUR STORY

Property assessments on our warehouses were continually increasing, even when the real estate market in our area indicated otherwise. It was time to take some action and take the law into our own hands. We did some research and settled on using an outside firm specializing in tax issues to make a review of our business properties. The result was a sizable reduction in our tax bill, resulting in savings of over $20,000 per year.

THE PROCESS

The road to a lower tax bill began with a call to the tax firm. We talked about the properties and our belief that the assessments were too high. The representative talked through the process and what they would need from us: property descriptions, locations, property tax bills, and recent appraisals, if available.

The tax firm sent a contract, which outlined the scope of the work and fee structure. Fees would be based on a percentage of the tax savings they could create, if any. If there was no tax reduction, there would be no cost to us for the assessment.

We sent the requested information to the firm, and shortly thereafter, they scheduled a visit to tour our properties. At the conclusion of the tour, we received a write-up on each of the properties indicating the assessment of value and a recommendation to file an appeal with the city taxing authority. For us, it made sense to move forward with the appeal.

Start to finish, the process took a few months, but only a few hours of our time. We did the initial phone call, reviewed the contract, gathered paperwork, and met the tax firm representative for the property tour. In the end, the reduction in our tax bill was $21,941 per year.

We saved a good deal of money in this process and you can too. Follow the steps to reduce your taxes and score one for the good guys.

REDUCE UTILITY COSTS

"Know the difference between your necessary and discretionary expenses."

-- *Alexa Von Tobel*

BEER DISTRIBUTORS HAVE BIG WAREHOUSES that need to be lit properly to allow for accurate product picking and a safe working environment. Keeping the warehouse brightly lit 24 hours a day costs some big dough, so it's always nice to discover a way to reduce expenses and get a better product or service in the bargain.

One such example is an LED retro-fit of your warehouse. Our business went through the process, saved over $100,000 in utility costs, and got better lighting in the bargain. Best of all, we only had to sign the paperwork and get out of the way – our contractor did all the heavy lifting.

The name of the game is to keep utility costs as low as possible through more energy efficient options. In financial terms, this means spending less money to achieve the same result -- all good things.

Lucky for beer distributors, many contractors specialize in providing energy efficient lighting options. Even better, these contractors work with your local utility company to get incentives and rebates. The result is improved lighting, lower utility bills, and a nice rebate from the electric company to offset the project cost.

As a result of our project, we saved $127,000. The total system cost, including labor, parts, and supplies, came to $26k before rebates. The total costs also include estimated ongoing maintenance and labor related to the lighting and fixtures. For us, the total return on the investment was 384%.

As an aside, we'll describe how to calculate the return on investment figure. Divide the estimated annual total savings by the total investment. To figure out the total project ROI, take the lifetime savings minus the total investment, then divide by the total investment. You'll be pleased with the result.

If you want to learn more and see what you can save, the process works like this:

1. Google search for "LED retrofit" to locate a contractor.
2. Your contractor will provide an overview of the process and helpful links so you can learn more than you ever cared to know about LEDs.
3. The actual meeting with the contractor is a quick discussion of the bullet points of the project as well as a "show and tell" of the lighting options. Be prepared for a blinding experience – don't look directly into the light.
4. To help your contractor calculate expected savings, you'll need to gather a few details: Get copies of the last few months'

electric bills and outline your warehouse hours of operations (times when the lights will be on).

5. Your contractor will then discuss potential utility rebates and any pros/cons. Lastly, the contractor will do a walk-through of your warehouse, take an inventory of the existing lighting, and discuss lighting needs (for example, more light or less light needed in certain areas). It is important to get the correct LED solution, i.e., the proper color and lumen output.
6. After the meeting, your contractor will put together a proposal, complete with project costs, anticipated utility rebates, and total project return on investment.

We invested a grand total of two hours to save well over $100,000. You can measure ROI however you'd like, but that's a pretty good use of time.

If you haven't taken advantage of an LED retro-fit, now is the time to do so. Follow the steps above, do a little research, and save big dough.

WRAP UP

List any ideas from this section that can help improve financial results in your beer business.

Write down an action plan: How and when to implement the idea.

Do it now before you forget or get busy with something else. Your income statement is counting on you.

- ☐ ______
- ☐ ______
- ☐ ______
- ☐ ______
- ☐ ______
- ☐ ______
- ☐ ______
- ☐ ______
- ☐ ______
- ☐ ______

FINANCING AND LOAN BASICS

INTRODUCTION TO BANKING AND FINANCING

THE BEER DISTRIBUTION BUSINESS REQUIRES a lot of capital investment. We have warehouses to store and safeguard the beer and a fleet of trucks to get it delivered. Additionally, we need tractors, trailers, forklifts, pallet jacks, racking, and countless other assets to keep the operation running smoothly. All this capital investment requires cash, which usually comes in the form of borrowing money.

In this chapter, we'll review financing and loan basics so that you are well-prepared to finance your beer business now and into the future.

Proper financing means you are prepared for good times and bad. It also means you'll have dry powder if an acquisition opportunity comes up as well as cash reserves if you hit financial bumps in the road. Overall, a good financing structure fortifies your business and provides financial stability.

In this section, we'll first look at common banking terms so you can speak the language of your banker. Then, we'll dig into how your banker thinks, what financial information they need from you, and who really makes the decisions on a loan.

As the beer business requires a lot of capital and cash, learning to get the best financing structure will position your company for solid growth into the future.

FINANCING BASICS FOR BEER DISTRIBUTORS

REGARDLESS OF HOW YOU FEEL about debt, borrowing money is just part of doing business as a beer distributor these days. It requires a lot of cash -- trucks, equipment, warehouses, and so on eventually need replacement or expansion.

Moreover, we may be presented with an opportunity to buy another distributor and need to learn about the pain and pleasure of acquisition financing. Or we may need to get a working capital line of credit to ride out the cash draining experience of the pre-summer inventory build. After all, if you're not growing, you're dying, and to grow, you need to borrow money.

This section is an introduction to financing basics - the nuts and bolts of borrowing money to finance your business growth. I'll go over some loan terminology, provide an example of a typical distributor financing arrangement, and give you the steps to gain a better understanding of your own company's financing situation.

So, let's begin. You know you have loans, but you may not know how they are structured, when they get paid off, or what the payment terms are. The first step is to familiarize yourself with your loan portfolio.

To understand your debt details, talk to your CFO or someone on your finance team, or have them prepare a summary of your loan details. For guidance, use the loan summary template; it contains the relevant details you'll want to know and provides a framework for questions to ask.

Example Financing Structure					
Date: Today					
Prepared by: Head Bean Counter					
Loan Description	**Current balance**	**Payment**	**Frequency**	**Rate**	**Term (months)**
Line of credit	$450,000.00	Interest only	Monthly	3.00%	12
Delivery truck	$84,000.00	$1,350.00	Monthly	3.75%	60
Warehouse	$1,350,000.00	$5,250.00	Monthly	4.75%	84

Another option is to book an appointment with your loan officer to have them walk you through each loan in detail. Your banker will have a commitment letter summarizing all of your loans and loan terms, which serves as an easy reference guide. This meeting is also a great opportunity to negotiate a better interest rate -- this is my favorite part. Have some fun; you'll learn something and save some money in the process.

Once you have a handle on what your debt looks like, it's helpful to understand some basic financing terms. This will arm you with knowledge of the fundamental building blocks of debt financing. As knowledge is power, you'll get control over that debt.

BASIC LOAN TERMS

These terms are basic and may already be common knowledge for you. Skim through and skip over anything you already understand.

- Loan to value: The amount the bank will loan you is related to the value of the asset they are lending against. For example, if you buy a $5 million warehouse, the bank won't lend you the whole amount, but will keep the loan to value ratio at about 80%. This means they will lend you 80% of the $5 million value, which is $4 million. The remainder is on you to supply in the form of equity.
- Principal: The amount borrowed on the loan or amount still outstanding.
- Interest: If you want to make yourself sick, look at how much interest you will pay over the course of the loan. Interest is the amount you pay for the privilege of borrowing money.
- Interest rate: The cost of borrowing expressed in a percentage. The interest rate gets multiplied by the outstanding principal to determine the interest you'll pay each month. A variety of benchmarks are used to establish the rate - the prime rate, LIBOR, or the bank's internal cost of funds rates. Rates may be expressed as "prime plus 125 basis points," for example. A basis point is one hundredth of a percent. So, if you want to sound like a banker, use words like "basis points" often. Your credit rating, collateral, and a variety of other factors influence the interest rate you get.
- P&I or principal and interest: Together, both make up the amount of your monthly payment on the loan. Just like on your home mortgage, the monthly payment stays the same each month, but the P&I fluctuates based on the remaining principal. Early in the loan, more of your payment goes to

paying the interest, while later in the loan, when the principal is lower, more goes toward the principal.

- Term: The length of time on the loan for which the interest rate is fixed.
- Amortization period: The time period to repay the loan. Sounds similar to the loan term, doesn't it? Sometimes it's different. For instance, you borrow that $4 million for the warehouse, and the bank calculates your payments based on a 20-year amortization schedule. This spreads the payments over a long period of time and makes them easier to handle. However, the bank won't fix that interest rate for 20 years; they'll only fix it for say, seven years - the loan term. So, the amortization period is 20 years, but the loan term is seven years. Typically, after the seven years are up, the loan will renew but at a different interest rate.
- Amortization schedule: Not many folks outside banking and finance use this word. Simply put, an amortization schedule is a re-payment schedule. It's a listing of all the payments you will make on the loan and how much is allocated to principal and interest each time you make a payment.
- Covenants: Promises you make to the bank in exchange for the loan. The bank wants to make sure you not only pay down the loan as you agreed to do, but they also want to ensure you maintain certain financial benchmarks along the way. Be very careful with covenants. The bank does not take it lightly when you break a promise.

These terms are helpful to communicating effectively with your banker and getting a better loan arrangement for your beer business.

Now that you have some grounding in the language of loans, we should dig into the details of how your banker thinks, what's important to them, and the financial information they need from you to write a loan.

LOAN BASICS: KNOW YOUR BANKER

"At its core, banking is not simply about profit, but about personal relationships."

-- Felix Rohatyn

WE BORROW A LOT OF money in our business, but do we really know who we are borrowing from and how the loan process works?

- Who are these banking people and what makes them tick?
- What information do bankers look at to determine whether we're a good credit risk?
- What information should we know to better understand whether the bank will be there to support us in good times and bad?

We can learn a lot about our banking partner to ensure a smooth relationship and get the best financing arrangement possible. After all, the beer business is all about relationships; we have great relationships with our breweries, our retailers, and our employees. It is a large part of what makes us successful. Therefore, it makes sense to consider what kind of relationship you have with your banker and your bank.

What do you really know about how your loan officer operates, what they look for when writing a loan, and who they go to for approval? Who else is involved in examining the business and making decisions about whether a loan gets approved?

If you're like most beer distributors, you know your banker well. You golf together, attend charitable events, and talk whenever you need a loan. However, you may not know your banker's boss or the boss' boss. And that's the problem - if you don't know these people higher up the banking food chain, they don't know you.

Aside from a set of financial statements and a one-page memo from the banker, your company is just a name on the bank's loan reports. As long as the loan gets approved on the expected terms, this arrangement works fine and you don't ask too many questions. As long as the bank gets paid when they expect, it works fine for them, and they don't ask too many questions either.

But what if something changes? Perhaps the business takes a downturn and profits turn to losses. Your company shows up on the "naughty" list at the bank. Then, there are problems making payments on the debt, and help is needed to re-structure the loan. Who is going to help you then?

Or consider a more positive situation, one where you want to buy another beer distributor and need to borrow a huge amount of money. The amount is far more than your banker is authorized to handle. What then?

The relationship is the thing

Let's assume all is fine in your business (as it probably is). Profits are solid, cash flow is good, the bank is happy with you and your numbers. Furthermore, you have no immediate needs for a big loan, and there's no big acquisition on the horizon. Now is the perfect time to build or strengthen your relationship with the key decision-makers at the bank.

First, who are these key decision-makers? If you don't know already, talk to your banker and find out. They will be happy to tell you, arrange lunch meetings and golf outings.

It sounds painful (four hours on a golf course with the credit guy from the bank?), but it's part of building the relationship. We do this all the time with our major suppliers and key customers, and we can benefit greatly by investing time with the key people at our bank. Plus, they pay for everything.

It doesn't always have to be four hours of golf. Our process is to set up an 11 am meeting to talk business for an hour, then go to lunch to get to know these folks personally. During the business meeting, we review numbers, goals, and objectives. We talk about the state of the industry and the direction of our business. We talk about our challenges and how the bank may be able to help. Then we go to lunch. We blend business with getting to know them personally.

In sum, these folks may be bankers, but they are people too, and people work better with people they know and trust. It's key to build relationships with key decision-makers at the bank. You're not just trying to make a new friend; you're strengthening a business partnership that will benefit your beer business and your financial statements.

LOAN BASICS: KNOW YOUR BANK

"Drive-in banks were established so cars today could see their real owners."

-- E.Joseph Crossman

HOW DO LOAN DECISIONS GET made in a bank? We'd like to think our lender will hear our financing needs, review the numbers, and write a loan with the terms we want. But it doesn't always work that way.

Most bankers have a loan authority limit, which determines how much they can approve for a loan on their own. The limit will vary depending on the size of the bank and the experience of the lender.

Ask your banker upfront their limit. This will let you know if you only have to deal with one person or whether more people up the bank food chain need to sign off on the loan.

Let's say an average banker has a lending limit of $2 million. If you need a loan for more, or the amount of your outstanding loans exceed this amount, your banker must ask others at the bank to approve the loan as well. Depending on the bank and the loan request, the decision process may include a series of committees: loan committee, senior loan committee, and a director loan committee. The takeaway is that your banker may not have the final say on approving the loan.

The key decision-makers, the ones who sit on these committees, hold the fate of your loan in their hands. If you played your cards right in the relationship building phase, then you've met some or all of these people. This is where that golf outing or the two-hour lunch comes back to reward you. Remember, bankers do business with people they know and trust. If you made a connection with the credit guy over a Cobb salad, he will remember you. That Cobb salad moment can go a long way toward a loan approval.

In terms of references, there are many books on financing and banking. One guide I would recommend is "Financing the Small Business" by Robert Sisson. Your business may not be small, but the guidance in this book will be a big help if you're interested in more details. If you're not into it, make your CFO read it and have them tell you the Cliff's Notes.

WRAP UP

How does the loan approval process work? Who are the key players? What is important to them?

Start by getting a working knowledge of how decisions are made. Ask your banker about their lending authority. Have them walk you through who else becomes involved in the loan process and who else will have to approve the loan.

Get to know the key players and let them get to know you. You'll get the most out of your banker and your bank by building relationships with the key decision-makers and understanding the inner workings of their institution.

This doesn't have to be a long conversation, but it is helpful to know who else will be deciding your future. Then, go to lunch with them for that Cobb salad.

LOANS AND LOAN STRUCTURES

SO FAR, WE'VE COVERED BASIC loan terms, how to build a relationship with your banker, and tips to learn more about the loan approval process at your bank. Now, we'll dig into the details of how specific loans work and present a typical financing structure for a beer distributor.

WORKING CAPITAL OR REVOLVING LINE OF CREDIT

This loan provides credit to smooth out the cash flow bumps of a seasonal business. For example, if you build and pay for inventory in early April, but sales don't increase until May, you may have a cash crunch for a period of time. The line of credit is available cash to continue paying bills until sales increase and the related receivables start coming in as cash.

The term of the line of credit may renew yearly or every two or three years. The credit remains open and available for you to draw upon as you need it. It may be linked to your checking account using a sweep to line arrangement. Think of this like over-draft protection on your personal checking account. Any over-drafts on the business account get taken care of by the line of credit.

Interest is charged on the outstanding balance, or the principal. However, unlike a regular commercial term loan, there is not a set monthly payment schedule. Interest charged accumulates on the outstanding balance, with the rate based on Prime or LIBOR. A typical one these days might be prime or LIBOR plus 1.5%. Additionally, there may be a requirement for the line to be paid down to zero for a period of time each year - say for 30 days out of a calendar year, the loan needs to remain at zero.

The amount you can borrow on the line of credit is determined by a few factors: how much you ask for, how much you really need, and how much collateral you have to support the loan. You can determine your needs by looking at your historical cash flows over the past few years and projecting upcoming needs. The bank looks to inventory and accounts receivable for the collateral on the loan. They may lend 50% to 60% of your total inventory value and 70% to 80% of your accounts receivable. Depending on the amount of those assets, this can be a good chunk of credit when you need it. As with any open-ended credit (like credit cards), you've got to be disciplined. Just because the bank will loan it to you, it doesn't mean you should spend it all.

COMMERCIAL TERM LOAN

This loan is used to purchase assets for your business. A typical distributor needs to buy and finance trucks, warehouse equipment, vehicles for the sales team, and office equipment. The re-payment term varies based on the type of asset being purchased. Typically, you'll see a five- to seven-year term for these types of assets. The terms vary as the bank tries to match the useful life of the asset to the length of the loan.

Interest rates are fixed for the term of the loan, while the rate itself can vary. In general, the shorter the term, the lower the interest rate.

The collateral for the loan will be the asset you purchase - trucks, equipment, etc. To secure an interest in the asset, the bank will hold the title to vehicles that are registered and make a UCC filing on other assets, such as warehouse equipment. The UCC filing basically puts a lien on the equipment so that you can't sell it without the bank's permission. Banks love to be protected, and collateral in the form of hard assets makes them feel safe and cozy. To make them feel even cozier, the bank only loans 70% to 80% of the purchase price of the asset. You need to cover the remaining amount as your equity in the asset.

Commercial term loans get paid down, or amortize, with regularly scheduled payments. The payment schedule, or amortization schedule, shows how much of each monthly payment goes toward interest and how much goes toward paying down the principal. The portion you pay toward interest is deductible on your income statement as an expense. The portion you pay toward the principal is not deductible though. You do get to write off the principal another way through depreciation expense, however.

EQUIPMENT LINE OF CREDIT

Though similar to a working capital line of credit; an equipment line of credit is used specifically to purchase equipment. Setting it up affords you immediate credit to purchase trucks, warehouse equipment, or other assets for your distribution business. No need to wait around for the bank to approve anything or fill out paperwork. This loan is pre-approved, and the capital is ready and waiting.

Once the equipment is purchased, interest is only charged on the outstanding balance. After a period of time, the equipment line of credit converts into a term loan with regular monthly principal and interest payments. This is also known as a commercial equipment term loan.

COMMERCIAL REAL ESTATE LOAN

This type of loan is used to finance the purchase of land, buildings, or warehouses. Banks typically write loans of 15 to 25 years on real estate, as they figure it's safe collateral. Unlike your new delivery truck that loses 20% of its value as soon as you take a delivery, your real estate is a safer bet to hang onto its value (at least as far as your bank is concerned). While your bank may write a 20-year loan for your real estate, they won't fix the interest rate for that long.

Here, we have the difference between the loan term and the amortization period. The bank may fix the interest rate for a period of 7 years and amortize the loan over 20 years. All this means is that they are writing the loan as if you will pay it off over 20 years, but after the fixed interest rate period expires (the end of the 7th year), the rate will change. This is something to be mindful of when you write those loans - we're in a great interest rate environment now, but it may not be so great when your fixed interest rate period comes up for renewal.

Interestingly, you can get a mortgage on your home with a 30-year fixed interest rate, but few banks fix the interest rate on a commercial real estate loan for longer than 7 years (unless you want to pay an absurdly high rate). The reason is that banks are able to package home mortgages and sell them on the secondary market. That didn't work out so well during the mortgage crisis, but the 30-year rates are available today just the same. Unfortunately, there's no secondary market for the loan on your warehouse so the bank usually holds on to the note and doesn't want to fix that rate too far in the future.

As with other assets, the amount the banks lend will usually be 70% to 80% of the value of the real estate. If it's a new loan, or a re-finance, you will need an appraisal by a bank-approved appraiser. This determines the value, and the bank lends based on this number. So, if you have got a $3 million appraisal, the bank would lend up to 80% or $2.4 million and you'll need to come up with the remainder. The remainder is your equity and serves as more protection for the bank, should there be a problem.

As a final note on commercial real estate, for tax reasons, distributors often set up a separate real estate company outside of their main distribution business to hold the real estate. This may be something to keep in mind as you learn more about your company's financing - there are loans that may exist on subsidiary companies, such as your real estate holding company.

WRAP UP + ACTION ITEMS

For beer distributors, borrowing money is part of doing business these days. We need the borrowing ability to finance trucks and equipment, a warehouse expansion, and perhaps an acquisition. Leverage financial knowledge, loan terms, and banking relationships as your banker can only take it so far on their own.

WRAP UP

ACTION ITEMS

List any ideas from this section that can help improve financial results in your beer business.

Write down an action plan: How and when to implement the idea.

Do it now before you forget or get busy with something else. Your income statement is counting on you.

- ☐ ______________________________
- ☐ ______________________________
- ☐ ______________________________
- ☐ ______________________________
- ☐ ______________________________
- ☐ ______________________________
- ☐ ______________________________
- ☐ ______________________________
- ☐ ______________________________
- ☐ ______________________________

CASH FLOW MANAGEMENT

INTRODUCTION TO CASH FLOW

EVERYONE LOVES CASH, BUT FEW beer distributors focus specifically on improving cash flow. The emphasis is sales growth first and everything else second. A distant second.

Although there's nothing wrong with sales growth -- it's critical to success and sustained viability -- it eats cash in the form of increased inventory, accounts receivable, and operating expenses. The key is to grow sales profitably and keep a close eye on its impact on cash flow. Positive cash flow is critical to ensure distributors can pay bills, re-invest in the business, and take dividends.

In this chapter, we'll cover basic steps to improve cash flow in your company while still growing the beloved sales line on the income statement. We'll also look at the art and science behind managing cash flow and provide simple tools so that you can track, measure, and improve the most important asset in your beer business: cash.

THE 10 LAWS OF BUSINESS

> *"Never take your eyes off the cash flow, because it's the life blood of business."*
>
> *- Richard Branson*

IN SIMPLE TERMS, CASH FLOW is the money that flows into and out of your business. It represents the money you collect from sales and the money you pay out to your suppliers and vendors.

We know cash is flowing in and out of the business all the time, but understanding how it works and predicting what it will be can be tricky. To begin, we'll look at the four pillars of cash flow. Once you understand these concepts, the rest will come easy.

1. Know the 10 laws of business
2. Understand there is a difference between profit and cash flow
3. Learn and use the 5 drivers of cash flow
4. Implement the Cash Flow System in your business

1. KNOW THE 10 LAWS OF BUSINESS

There are only 10 laws in business: 1) Don't run out of cash, 10) don't run out of cash, and all the rules in between don't mean crap. After all, cash is the fuel that drives your business. Your car won't go forward without fuel, and neither will your business. While you're growing sales, acquiring hot new brands, and building out the sales teams, remember that positive cash flow is king.

2. UNDERSTAND THAT CASH FLOW AND PROFIT ARE NOT THE SAME

Cash flow and profit can differ greatly. For one, the income statement may indicate a healthy profit, but it doesn't indicate positive cash flow. In fact, many profitable companies have no cash, and some unprofitable companies have plenty of cash. This seems unusual, but not when you understand that profit and cash flow are different.

The P&L records revenue and expense as transactions happen. Sales are recorded when product is delivered, while expenses are recorded when they are incurred and when we have an obligation to pay. However, the cash side of these transactions - when the customer pays for the product or when we pay our invoices – often occurs at a different time.

For example, we record a sale on the P&L when the product is delivered, but the cash isn't recorded until the customer pays. Collecting payment on the sale may take days, weeks, or even months. In some cases, the cash is never received at all, and we have a bad debt. A sale doesn't count as positive cash flow until the customer pays, and the check clears the bank. This is one disconnect between profit and cash flow.

Another disconnect has to do with inventory. We purchase inventory and store it in our warehouse until it's ordered by and delivered to the customer. The cash is gone as soon as we pay for the inventory, but we don't record an expense until we sell the inventory to the customer. The cash flow is lowered to pay for the inventory, but the expense on the P&L is unaffected.

We've been taught that the bottom line on the income statement is the measure of a business' performance. Profit is good, and losses are bad. While this is a good measure, we need to look at cash flow as well. The cash flow doesn't always follow the profit.

3. LEARN AND USE THE 5 DRIVERS OF CASH FLOW

In the beer distribution business, five primary areas impact your cash flow. Watch these key items closely to master cash flow.

1. Accounts receivable: Cash due from customers or suppliers that hasn't been collected yet.
2. Inventory: Product on the warehouse floor, waiting patiently to be sold to your customers.
3. Accounts payable: Cash due to suppliers and vendors that hasn't been paid yet.
4. Capital expenses: Big ticket items – trucks, cars, warehouse equipment.
5. Operating performance (profit): Net income or the bottom line on the income statement.

Note that only one of the cash flow drivers listed above is related to P&L (operating performance). All the others are related to the balance sheet.

The balance sheet doesn't get a lot of attention during the monthly financial reporting. To master cash flow, you'll need to give the balance sheet some love because cash flow is heavily influenced by what happens here.

We'll dig into each of these cash flow drivers in the next section, but for now, review the list and recognize how much of your cash flow depends on your balance sheet accounts.

4. IMPLEMENT A CASH FLOW SYSTEM IN YOUR BUSINESS

Three of my favorite words: cash flow + system. Put them together and it's like Batman and Robin, an unstoppable superhero team.

A system is defined as an organized method to achieve a predictable result. A cash flow system, in particular, is a step-by-step method you can implement in your business to keep on top of your cash flow drivers and increase cash flow.

In summary, a cash flow system includes these steps:

1. Know the score. Use a metric to track how well you are doing with each cash flow driver. For example, the Days on Hand in inventory or Days Sales Outstanding in accounts receivable.
2. Educate your team on what the metric is and how it's calculated. Show your employees how they can make a difference and improve the result.
3. Set a goal to improve the score, the metric. Use industry benchmarks or benchmark against past company performance as the goal. Communicate the goal to those who can influence the outcome.

4. Monitor the score, track progress towards the goal, and provide regular updates to your team.
5. Celebrate the win. When you hit the goal, take a moment to celebrate and praise the team. Free beer works well here.

So, there you have it, the four pillars of cash flow and a system to monitor results. As cash flows in and out of your business all the time, a cash flow system helps you measure and improve your most important asset: cash.

THE 5 DRIVERS OF CASH FLOW AND HOW TO MANAGE THEM

IN THIS SECTION WE'LL GO into the details of primary cash flow drivers for the beer distribution business. We'll also provide specific examples of how the Cash Flow System can be implemented so you can put more cash in the bank.

In beer distribution, five primary areas drive your cash flow:

1. Accounts receivable
2. Inventory
3. Accounts payable
4. Capital expenses
5. Operating Profit

CASH FLOW DRIVER 1: ACCOUNTS RECEIVABLE (A/R)

Accounts receivable are uncollected sales. You've bought the inventory, delivered it to the retailer, and now you need to collect the cash. Many states have credit laws that require retailers to pay you within a certain time period.

For example, Vermont is a cash-on-delivery state, while New Hampshire gives retailers 15 days to pay. In New Hampshire, if the retailer doesn't pay in the required time frame, they are put on a "list" and unable to purchase beer from any other distributor until the invoice is paid. I always liked that rule.

Keeping on top of your A/R is a critical piece to mastering your cash flow. A first step is to determine if you are collecting the money fast enough – the Days Sales Outstanding (DSO) calculation is a helpful measurement.

The DSO calculation works like this: Divide your accounts receivable by your average daily sales. For example, if sales were $3,000,000 in June, a month with 30 days, your average daily sales are $100,000. If your A/R balance is $2,000,000, divide this by $100,000 (average daily sales) and the result is 20 Days Sales Outstanding. There are many variations on this calculation (you can use selling days instead of calendar days), but the key is to be consistent.

Key Measurement: Days Sales Outstanding (DSO) Calculation			
			Key Notes
Accounts Receivable divided by Average Daily Sales			Shows how quickly your customers pay.
			Sales growth = growth in A/R
A/R Balance	$250,000		Growth in A/R = Longer time to get the cash
Average Daily Sales	$10,000		...that giant sucking sound is cash getting sucked into a/r...
Days Sales Outstanding (DSO)	**25.0**		DSO: Compare this to the payment terms you give your customers

Action items to master your accounts receivable:

1. Calculate your current Days Sales Outstanding in A/R, compare it against industry benchmarks or your past DSO number, and set a goal to improve.
2. Communicate the goal to everyone who can make an impact on improving the number – the sales team, drivers, and

merchandisers, if appropriate. It takes a village to collect the money. Engage the villagers.

3. Establish a regular routine to monitor the progress towards the A/R goal. A daily email from your credit manager or finance person with the DSO calculation helps to keep on top of the number.
4. Hire the right person. Many people do not like to collect money, but a select few love it. Find those people, get them into the collection role, and turn them loose.

CASH FLOW DRIVER #2: INVENTORY

Inventory is the lifeblood of a distribution business, but if not managed properly, it will drain your cash flow. A typical beer distributor will spend 70% of sales volume on inventory purchases – for many wholesalers this can be tens of millions of dollars.

With so many brands and SKUs to manage, it's easy to lose track of your inventory numbers and how much you have on hand. Seasonal products, line extensions, and the myriad of package sizes have contributed to the infamous SKU proliferation. Keeping on top of your inventory value has never been more important.

Inventory Days on Hand (DOH) is a helpful metric to calculate whether inventory is eating up too much of your cash flow. The measurement can be applied to your inventory as a whole or to individual suppliers, brands, and packages to identify where you're running heavy.

The calculation works like this: Divide your inventory balance by your average daily cost. If your cost of sales is $2,250,000 in June, a 30-day month, your average daily cost of sales is $75,000. If your inventory value is $3,000,000, divide this by $75,000, and the result is 40 Days on Hand.

Key Measurement: Inventory Days on Hand (DOH)			
Inventory Days on Hand = Inventory divided by Forecasted Sales			
Days On Hand (DOH)			**Key Notes**
Inventory on Hand	10,000	Cases	Shows whether you have too much / too little inventory
Daily Forecasted Sales	500	Cases	How efficiently you are managing inventory
DOH Score	20	Days	Compare to historical average
DOH Goal	10	Days	Compare to industry benchmarks

Action items to master your inventory

1. Calculate your Days on Hand, compare it to industry benchmarks, set a goal to improve.
2. Communicate the goal to those on your team who can make a difference. Usually this is the inventory manager, the general manager, and the sales team.
3. Establish a regular routine to monitor your Days on Hand and progress toward your goal.
4. Walk the warehouse. Reports are one thing, but seeing the inventory (the money) sitting in the warehouse will make a difference. Talk to your warehouse people and ask questions. What problems do they see? Are there brands that just aren't moving? Are there packages more susceptible to breakage? Get their input. The answers may surprise you.

CONCLUSION

Accounts receivable and inventory can have a huge impact on cash flow. Start by reviewing them in your company. Implement the ideas and action items presented here -- I can already feel the cash flow improving in your business.

HOW TO MANAGE ACCOUNTS PAYABLE AND CAPITAL EXPENSES

CASH FLOW DRIVER #3: ACCOUNTS PAYABLE (A/P)

ACCOUNTS PAYABLE ARE YOUR UNPAID invoices. You've ordered inventory, received it, and now you need to pay out the cash. From a cash perspective, accounts payable is "money out," while accounts receivable is known as "money in." Managing your money out is as important, if not more important, than watching the money coming in.

At a typical wholesaler, the purchasing process involves a lot of people and paperwork. There is an approval process to ensure expenses are authorized before cash gets paid out. Purchase orders are created and approved, products or services are received, and invoices are reviewed and approved to be paid. The invoice then goes to the accounts payable department for payment.

The accounts payable team is the last line of defense before an invoice is processed and paid. It's their job to make sure all the proper approvals are in place and the paperwork matches up. Millions of dollars flow through your A/P department each year, so carefully managing and monitoring your "money out" process is critical to cash flow.

A first step is to determine if you are paying your invoices too quickly. The Average Days to Pay calculation is a useful measurement; it works like this:

1. Determine your average A/P balance for the month (beginning of month A/P + end of month A/P divided by 2).
2. Multiply by the number of days in that month.
3. Divide this by the total purchases for the month.

For example, let's say you had average A/P of $1,200,000 in the month of June and total purchases of $1,500,000. You'd multiply the A/P by 30 days, and then divide the result by the total of your purchases: $36,000,000 (which is $1,200,000 x 30) divided by $1,500,000 equals 24. This means you're paying your bills in 24 days on average.

On its own, this number doesn't mean much. You'll need to look at your vendor terms and determine if you're paying too quickly. If most of your vendors give you 30-day terms, then in the example above, you're paying too quickly and paying out cash before you need to.

Plenty of factors can influence the average days to pay number (paying bills early to take early pay discounts, certain vendors who require COD payment, etc.), but this can be a useful benchmark to determine how well you are managing accounts payable. For better cash flow, the higher the number of Average Days to Pay, the better.

Key Measurement: Average Days to Pay A/P			
Avg Days to Pay A/P			**Key Notes**
Avg A/P balance	$200,000		Shows whether you are paying your vendors too quickly
x Number of days in month	30		Measures how efficiently you manage your accounts payable (cash out)
	$6,000,000		Compare the Avg Days to Pay to the terms your vendor gives you
Divide by Purchases in Month	$350,000		If this number is too low, you're paying too fast
Avg Days to Pay	**17**		When you pay too fast, you're hurting cash flow

ACTION ITEMS TO MANAGE YOUR ACCOUNTS PAYABLE

1. Calculate your Average Days to Pay – how many days you take on average to pay your invoices.
2. Review your supplier and vendor payment terms - do your vendors give you 30 days to pay, but you're paying in 20?
3. Set a goal to improve your Average Days to Pay and communicate it to your team. The A/P manager will have the most control over this number as they are the last line of defense before cash is paid out.
4. Examine your invoice approval and payment process. Who can approve a payment? Are they really looking at what money goes out?
5. Personally review every invoice that gets paid. You will be amazed at the stuff you're paying for.

Side note: Your vendors may offer a 1% or 2% discount if the bill is paid within 10 days. You'll sacrifice short-term cash flow, but the return on investment can be an annualized 12% to 24% -- not a bad return on investment.

CASH FLOW DRIVER #4: CAPITAL EXPENSES (CAPEX)

Capital expenses are those "big ticket" purchases like delivery trucks, forklifts, and warehouse improvements. These purchases are expensive (over $5,000 for example) and have a useful life of more than one year.

CAPEX are recorded as assets on the balance sheet. The cost of these items gets expensed as depreciation each year over their useful life. The idea is to spread the cost of the purchase over the useful life of the asset.

For example, a forklift might cost $35,000 and have a useful life of seven years (as defined by the IRS). You'll pay the cash today, assuming you don't finance or lease the purchase, but you won't expense the item until it is depreciated. The cash is gone, but the expense isn't recorded on the income statement until depreciation is recorded.

Due to the many large expenses, the beer distribution business is very capital intensive - lots of iron and bricks. Delivery trucks need to be replaced on a schedule, new laptops and IT equipment needs to be purchased, and the warehouse regularly needs improvements. All of these purchases are necessary to keep up with growth, but they also suck up cash.

Keeping on top of your CAPEX is critical to mastering your cash flow. A first step is to determine how efficiently you are using your assets using the Return on Assets (ROA) calculation, a useful measurement indicating the return your company can generate with the assets it has.

The calculation works like this: Return on Assets = Net Income divided by Total Assets. Simple enough, right? For example, if your Net Income is $1,000,000 and your Total Assets are $10,000,000, you have a 10% Return on Assets.

Key Measurement: Return on Assets			
...and Return on Investment			
Return on Assets (ROA)			**Key Notes**
Net Income	$20,000		Measures how efficiently you are using assets (cash)
Divided by			Looks at total net income compared to total
Total Assets	$450,000		cash invested in assets
Equals ROA	4%		

Action items to manage your capital expenses

1. Calculate your Return on Assets.
2. Review your capital budget. Plan when you make the purchases and determine the impact on cash flow. Review the Return on Assets calculation with your team as you plan the capital budget.
3. Set up an equipment line of credit with your bank. Negotiate a good interest rate so you have the funding available to purchase trucks, equipment, and other assets.
4. Lease vs. buy. Look at options for leasing, instead of purchasing an asset. Leasing can take the stress off cash flow and leverage the expertise of a leasing company. Wholesalers are in not only the beer business but also the leasing business. Take advantage of what these vendors have to offer.

Breathe in all the goodness. That's the scent of cash flow improving in your business.

HOW TO MANAGE OPERATING PERFORMANCE (PROFIT)

IN THIS SECTION, WE'LL LOOK at the final cash flow driver, Operating Performance (profit), and provide specific examples of how the Cash Flow System can be implemented in your company to increase the number. Strap on the seat belt, the road to better cash flow is straight ahead.

CASH FLOW DRIVER #5: OPERATING PERFORMANCE (PROFIT)

The Cash Flow system is made up of five key steps you can apply to most any aspect of your business. Here's a quick overview of the steps and how to apply them to managing company profit.

1. Know the score: Start with the building blocks of profit: sales, gross margin, and operating expenses. Sales minus the cost of sales (purchases, freight, taxes) equals margin, while margin minus operating expenses equals your profit.

Most route accounting systems make it easy to run reports on these key numbers. Set up a book of reports, run them regularly, and share them out to members of your team.

2. Educate your team: Providing your team with key numbers is a good start. Next, show them what the numbers mean, how the calculations work, and how employees can make a difference in improving the score. For instance, many salespeople I've worked with in the past had no idea about gross profit.

Teach your sales team about numbers beyond the sales line. Show them how gross profit is calculated. You'll open their eyes, and give them the knowledge they need to help improve the score.

3. Set a goal to improve the score: Start with the bottom line first. Identify what you need for profit and work backwards from there. When you begin with the end in mind, you can create a Profit Plan designed to achieve your most important goal: profit. When you increase profit, you increase cash flow. Everyone wins.

As with the other cash flow drivers, it is helpful to create metrics to manage your sales, margins, and operating expenses. Percentages work well here, as you'll only need to focus on three or four numbers to understand where you stand in relation to the plan. Below is an example:

Sample Profit plan:

- Sales forecasted at 3.5% growth over prior year
- Margin 25% of sales
- Operating Expense 20% of sales
- Profit 5% of sales

With a summary profit plan using percentages, you only need to look at these four numbers to see how you're doing (instead of the dozens of pages and line items on your financial reports). Keep it simple, use percentages.

4. Monitor the score and track progress: Keep your team updated on company results. Weekly meetings to review financial information work well. This is an opportunity for different department supervisors to interact and share information. If the team knows the score, they are in a better position to improve results.

5. Celebrate the win. People want to make a difference in the world. When the team hits a goal, celebrate the achievement. It may not seem like a big deal, but it can mean the world to your employees. Take a moment to acknowledge what was accomplished and reinforce the importance of the goal.

Action Steps to Manage Profit and Master the Art of Cash Flow:

1. Know the score. Use numbers and metrics to track company results – sales, gross margins, operating expenses and the bottom line. Share the numbers with your team – those who can improve the score.
2. Educate your team on what the numbers mean and how metrics are calculated. Show your employees how they can make a difference and improve the result.
3. Set a goal to improve the score. Setup a Profit Plan and benchmark against past company performance. Communicate the goal to those who can influence the outcome.
4. Monitor the score, track progress, and provide regular updates to your team.
5. Celebrate the win. When you hit the goal, praise the team and hand out free t-shirts. Everyone loves t-shirts.

CASH IS KING

Accounts receivable, accounts payable, inventory, capital expenditures and operating performance all have a big impact on your cash flow and need to be closely monitored and managed.

This chapter presented specific, actionable steps you can implement in your company to improve cash flow: Know the 10 laws of business, recognize the difference between profit and cash flow, learn the five drivers of cash flow, and implement the cash flow system.

Now you have the knowledge and the tools. Get out there, take action, and improve cash flow in your business.

WRAP UP

ACTION ITEMS

List any ideas from this section that can help improve financial results in your beer business.

Write down an action plan: How and when to implement the idea.

Do it now before you forget or get busy with something else. Your income statement is counting on you.

- ☐ ______________________________
- ☐ ______________________________
- ☐ ______________________________
- ☐ ______________________________
- ☐ ______________________________
- ☐ ______________________________
- ☐ ______________________________
- ☐ ______________________________
- ☐ ______________________________
- ☐ ______________________________

INVENTORY MANAGEMENT BEST PRACTICES

INTRODUCTION TO INVENTORY MANAGEMENT

BEER INVENTORY PURCHASES ARE YOUR biggest outlay of cash each year. A $100 million revenue beer wholesaler will purchase $70mm in inventory each year. That is a lot of cheese.

Do you have a solid inventory ordering team? Do you have a warehouse team who is trained and skilled in making inventory counts? Have you "safeguarded" the inventory, otherwise your biggest asset on the balance sheet?

Now, more than ever, you need a great inventory team and inventory management system to manage your SKUs. The keywords here are management and inventory. You need to actively, aggressively and decisively manage inventory, or it will crush your cash flow. So many new brands and SKUs come in every day that it's challenge to keep on top of it all.

In this chapter, we'll review the key inventory metrics you'll need to calculate and show you how to use those metrics to create a scoreboard to measure and manage your biggest asset. We'll also look at a tool you can use to identify under-performing items in your inventory portfolio.

As your inventory is your biggest use of cash, let's learn how to manage that asset and gain control over all those SKUs.

SKU MANAGEMENT

> *"The more inventory a company has, the less likely they have what they need."*
>
> *- Taiichi Ohno*

IT USED TO BE A lot simpler. Just a few decades ago, beer wholesalers carried 100 SKUs on average. Today, the average is well over 1,000. A ten-fold increase in a short period of time.

In addition to SKU count growth, the number of craft breweries has increased five-fold in the last ten years from 1,500 to over 7,000.

The growth in both areas has created a phenomenon called SKU "intensity" – the increase in package types per brand. In the past, a beer brand might be available in half-barrels and 4/6 pack bottles.

Today, beer is being packaged in 12oz cans, 16oz cans, 6 packs, 12 packs, 15 packs, and so on. You might have five or ten different packages for the same beer. Now, that's intense.

Non-beer SKUs are also being added to the mix: wine, non-alcohol, and snacks, for example. These fill up the delivery truck and can help get you more profitable stops; however, they also fill up the warehouse and create additional challenges to manage the inventory.

So how did this happen?

Consumers demand a wide variety of choices. They want what's new and what's different. To keep up, distributors have to take on new breweries, new packages, and new styles. New and different drives the growth of SKUs in your portfolio. The simpler times of consumer brand loyalty is on a hiatus.

Distributors and retailers are scrambling to meet the new demands, and managing inventory by FOMO (fear of missing out)on the next big thing. As a result, distributors take on more brands, the SKU count goes up, and your cash flow goes down.

DISTRIBUTOR EVOLUTION

In response to all this change, distributors have needed to evolve. Specialized sales teams have been added to focus on craft beer. Sophisticated warehouse and inventory systems have been installed to keep track of all the new SKUs. Moreover, higher skills and new training for employees has been needed to keep pace with these new systems.

Change is nothing new for distributors, as the evolution of the beer business has been constant. The SKU challenge presents one more in a series of changes.

SKU CARRYING COSTS

So, let's get into the nitty gritty: What is the cost to your business of these SKU increases? In other words, how much more does it cost if you have 500 SKUs or 1,000? How about 1,500 SKUs or 5,000?

To answer the question, we'll begin with an assessment and calculation of Cost to Carry Inventory. This metric captures all costs included in managing, maintaining, and holding your inventory.

Interestingly, studies show that 65% of companies don't calculate carrying costs. If you don't know yours, it is difficult to manage and improve them.

The main purpose of calculating your Cost to Carry Inventory is to identify controllable costs and use this information as a basis for making decisions on managing your inventory portfolio of breweries, brands, and SKUs.

SKU CARRYING COSTS: RULES OF THUMB

The average cost to carry inventory is 25% of inventory value. The number varies greatly from company to company, with percentages ranging from 18 to 75%.

The calculation works like this: Add up all the expenses to manage, maintain, and hold your inventory and then divide it by the average on-hand inventory value. For example, Total Costs to Carry ($500,000) divided by Inventory Value of ($2,000,000) = 25%

SKU CARRYING COSTS: WHAT'S INCLUDED

Below is a listing of costs typically included in the Cost to Carry Inventory calculation:

- Rent/Lease expense
- Utilities
- Wages: Operations Team
- Wages: Admin Team
- Breakage, Out of Code, Shrinkage
- Destruction Costs
- Insurance
- Depreciation
- Cost of capital (interest)
- Transportation/Handling
- Taxes

SKU CARRYING COST TEMPLATE

To create your schedule of carrying costs, follow the steps below:

1. List out costs associated with holding inventory. Use the list above, add/subtract based on the specifics of your beer business.
2. Identify the basis for the cost – factors that drive the cost. For example, hours and labor rates drive the wages, and square footage drives lease costs.
3. Quantify the total annual cost for each item.
4. Identify fixed costs and variable costs. Fixed costs are those that stay the same if you have 100 SKUs or 1,000. Variable costs increase or decrease depending on the amount of inventory.
5. Highlight costs you can control/reduce.
6. Calculate and input your average on-hand inventory value.

Inventory Carrying Cost Model	***Numbers***
Interest Expense	$110,500
Average value of inventory on hand	$3,400,000
Interest rate	3.25%
Administrative expense	$60,000
Total Admin/Inventory ordering labor expense	$60,000
Ordering / Logistics / Tracking	
New Product setup	
Warehouse Labor expense	$200,000
Total Warehouse labor expense	$200,000

SKU CARRYING COSTS: HARD COSTS VS. SOFT COSTS

The items above are Hard Costs, or the actual dollars, spent on carrying inventory. There are soft costs to consider as well.

Soft Costs:

- Opportunity costs: These are the loss of potential gains when one alternative is chosen over another. We have finite resources, so when dollars are invested in one brand or one SKU, they aren't available to invest in something else (other brands, other business opportunities, etc.)
- Focus costs: The sales team can only handle so much; overload, distraction, and confusion costs money. Too many SKUs and brands can become too much to focus on.

Soft costs are difficult to quantify and don't show up clearly on the income statement, but they do affect the price you pay to manage inventory.

SKU INVENTORY METRICS

Management of inventory can become a game of don't run out, but don't have too much on hand. It's helpful to set proper expectations and use numbers to measure those expectations.

SKU Inventory Metrics help to quantify what good inventory management looks like. While there are dozens of ways to measure inventory, we'll boil them down to these Four Key Metrics:

1. Days on Hand. Measures "Don't have too much."
2. Out of Stocks. Measures "Don't run out."
3. Out of Code. Watch and manage code dates.
4. Inventory Variances. Count and safeguard your inventory.

In the next section, we'll show you how to calculate and communicate these numbers to your team.

INVENTORY SCOREBOARD - KEY METRICS

"If you torture the data long enough it will confess."

- Ronald Coase

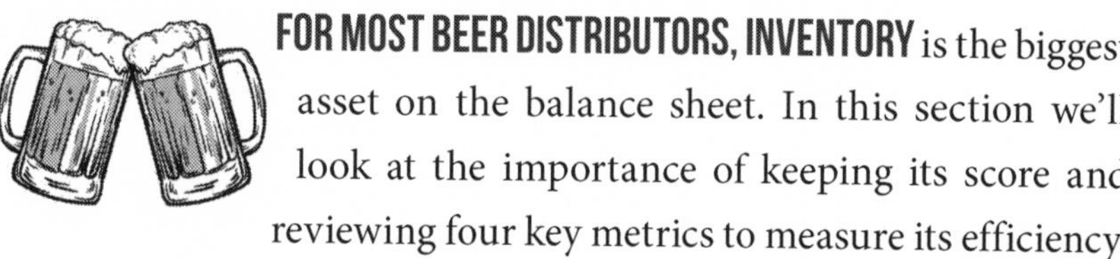

FOR MOST BEER DISTRIBUTORS, INVENTORY is the biggest asset on the balance sheet. In this section we'll look at the importance of keeping its score and reviewing four key metrics to measure its efficiency.

All members of your inventory team should review and understand the metrics below. The score should be posted in the warehouse, office, lunchroom, wherever the team can see the numbers. Don't hide the numbers on a spreadsheet on someone's laptop. Share the score so that you can improve inventory and the bottom line on the income statement.

The Inventory Scoreboard: Four Key Metrics of Inventory Management

1. Days on Hand
2. Out of Stocks
3. Out of Code
4. Inventory Variances

INVENTORY DAYS ON HAND (DOH)

Imagine your inventory as piles of cash stacked around the warehouse. Big piles of dollar bills, shrink-wrapped and stacked floor to ceiling on pallets. The goal is to keep only as much cash tied up in product as is necessary to satisfy market demand. The inventory days on hand metric measures how efficiently inventory is managed.

Too much inventory leads to problems: a drain on cash flow, using up premium warehouse space, and stale dated products. Inventory days on hand tells us how many days sales of inventory we have sitting in the warehouse.

For example, if we have 3,000 cases of Bud Light 30 pack cans and we forecast to sell 300 per day on average, then we have 10 days' worth of product on hand (3,000 cases on hand divided by 300 case sales per day = 10 days of inventory). Therefore, Inventory Days on Hand = Inventory divided by Forecasted Sales.

How much inventory is too much? Compare the days on hand number with how long it takes to get product from the supplier. Ideally, the days on hand will match up with the lead time to get new product. If the days on hand metric is significantly higher than the order lead time, you have too much. Set a goal for your inventory days on hand and track your results against it.

OUT OF STOCKS (OOS)

Few things irritate an owner or sales manager more than out of stock inventory. These are literally lost sales. "There is no reason we should be out of stock on XYZ product!" cries the sales manager. But of course, there's always a reason. Out of stocks occur in many ways. Below are four of the main causes:

1. Sales forecast: Inventory is ordered based on projected sales. If sales greatly exceed the projection, we run out of product, and incur out of stocks.
2. Supplier delivery: The amount delivered is less than what was ordered. It happens, particularly with high-demand products from craft breweries that can't keep up.
3. Inventory variances: The amount on the floor is less than what the computer says. The shortage is due to mis-picks, theft, or unrecorded stale product.
4. Communication: It's key in any relationship, but particularly important between inventory manager and sales manager. Bad forecasts, supplier shortages, and inventory variances occur regularly and should be communicated. Poor communication leads to out of stocks, plain and simple.

Out of stocks are part of doing business, but when they occur, they can be damaging. Measuring this key metric, sharing the information with the team, and tasking them with improving the number are important parts of the inventory management plan.

You can measure and report out of stocks as a percentage of sales in dollars or cases. For example, if the sales goal for the month is $1,000,000 and the out of stock goal is half a percent, the out of stock dollar goal is $5,000 ($1mm x 0.005). Each day, the amount of sales and out of stocks can be computed, turned into an out of stock percentage, and compared against the goal. The team will know the score and where they stand in relation to the goal -- Out of Stock Goal = Total out of stocks ($) divided by Sales ($).

Post the out of stock score in the office, in the warehouse, and in the sales meeting room. This allows the team to be in a position to immediately respond and make changes if the score is coming up short. No need to wait until the end of the week or end of the month to know where things stand.

Provide training on what the goal is, how to calculate it, and where to find the score. The important part is up to the team - identify where and why the score is falling short and get it back on track.

OUT OF CODE (OOC)

Out of code is the death of your inventory, and death is final. With the increased competition at retail, and increased quantities of inventory held in warehouses, distributors are seeing more out of code product than ever.

Preventing out of code product is the goal. This requires a good plan to manage product, including proper rotation and moving product from slow to faster moving retail accounts (where legal to do so). Many distributors have detailed OOC prevention plans, and some use incentives to focus employees on reducing out of code product.

One calculation you can use to measure out of code is to divide OOC product by the total sales during a month or quarter (Out of Code product (cases) divided by Sales (cases) = OOC %). This provides an out of code percentage in relation to total sales. For example, if you sell 100,000 cases in a month and 400 cases go out of code, the percentage is 0.4% (400 divided by 100,000 = 0.4%).

Remember, what gets measured gets managed. We measure so we can manage the out of code, improve on the number, and improve results on the income statement.

There are two flavors of out of code inventory: warehouse OOC and retail OOC. Each should be measured and have its own OOC prevention plan.

1. Warehouse out of code: Product that never had a chance to fulfill its dream. It sits in the warehouse from birth to death and never gets delivered to retail. This can be controlled through rotation, code date monitoring, and communication to the sales team. Many warehouses have a close code section, where inventory is segregated, easily identified, and can get special treatment - moving this out to a retailer that can sell the product quickly.
2. Retail out of code: Product at retail that doesn't sell through to the consumer. All sales are not final. If the product goes out of code in the account, it is usually the distributor's responsibility to pick up and credit the account. The sales and delivery teams are in and out of the retail account weekly and should monitor code dates.

Out of code product is a growing expense line on the income statement. Set up regular measurements of out of code, communicate it to the team, and work to reduce the number. And of course, make sure you comply with relevant state and federal regulations.

INVENTORY VARIANCES

An inventory variance is the difference between inventory on the warehouse floor and the computer inventory. A variety of things cause these variances: mis-picked product, breakage that doesn't get recorded, theft, errors from previous inventory counts, and so on.

Many small mistakes can add up to big dollars and big variances in your inventory. This can have a corrosive effect on the entire distributor organization as well as lead to out of stocks, poor customer service, and mistrust of inventory accuracy by employees.

To get a handle on inventory variances, start with a measurement of overall inventory accuracy. There are many ways to do this, but I've found this calculation to be useful: Inventory variance (cases) divided by total inventory on the floor (cases) = inventory variance %.

When you conduct a count of inventory, simply divide the total variance by the total cases on the floor. For example, if the computer inventory indicates 100,000 cases of product, but the physical count shows only 99,000 cases, there is a 1,000 case difference, and 1,000 cases divided by 100,000 cases = 1% inventory variance. You can compute this for the total inventory (as in the example above) or by individual SKU.

THE INVENTORY SCOREBOARD

Inventory is the biggest asset on the balance sheet, so give it the time and attention it deserves. Use this template to set up an inventory scoreboard so that you can improve profitability in your beer business.

1. Days on Hand
2. Out of Stocks
3. Out of Code
4. Inventory Variances

Remember the old business adage: What gets measured gets managed. Set a goal, measure your inventory, and improve the score. It's a win for your company, your customers, and your income statement.

Inventory Scoreboard		
Days On Hand (DOH)		
Inventory on Hand	100,000	Cases
Daily Forecasted Sales	4,000	Cases
DOH Score	25	Days
DOH Goal	20	
Inventory Days on Hand = Inventory divided by Forecasted Sales		
Out of Stocks (OOS)		
Out of Stocks YTD	$15,000	
Sales YTD	$1,000,000	
OOS %	1.5%	
OOS Goal	1.0%	
Out of Stock Goal = Total out of stocks ($) divided by Sales ($)		
Out of Code (OOC)		
Out of Code YTD	1,400	Cases
Sales YTD	50,000	Cases
OOC %	2.80%	
OOC Goal	2.00%	
Out of Code product (cases) divided by Sales (cases) = OOC %		
Inventory Count Variances		
Inventory Count Variances	900	Cases
Total Inventory on Floor	100,000	Cases
Variance %	0.90%	
Variance goal	1.00%	
Inventory variance (cases) divided by total inventory on the floor (cases) = inventory variance %		

ACTION ITEMS

List any ideas from this section that can help improve financial results in your beer business.

Write down an action plan: How and when to implement the idea.

Do it now before you forget or get busy with something else. Your income statement is counting on you.

- ☐ ______________________________
- ☐ ______________________________
- ☐ ______________________________
- ☐ ______________________________
- ☐ ______________________________
- ☐ ______________________________
- ☐ ______________________________
- ☐ ______________________________
- ☐ ______________________________
- ☐ ______________________________

COMPENSATION PLANNING

INTRODUCTION TO COMPENSATION PLANNING

AFTER THE COST OF INVENTORY, payroll expense is the biggest line item on your income statement. And it's by far the biggest operating cost for your business.

Every department has employees and managers - sales, merchandisers, delivery, warehouse, and administration. These folks need to get paid, or they won't show up to work. Additionally, they need to be paid well, or they'll go to work somewhere else. The cost of employee turnover is rarely measured in the financial statements, but it's a real cost just the same.

Keep in mind employee compensation is a huge expense. Therefore, compensation planning is hugely important so that you achieve the best possible financial results.

As we are in a regulated industry, check the relevant state and federal regulations to ensure your compensation plan is in compliance.

In this section, we'll review strategies to focus your training efforts on the most important parts of the job; this is the 80/20 of employee training. Second, we'll review the key components of basic compensation planning and cover the one rule that you must follow in your plan. Third, we'll finish up with the Compensation Planning Checklist, which you can reference to ensure all the important questions have been addressed and answered.

Don't leave payroll expense and compensation planning to chance. Read on to learn how to build the perfect plan for employees in your beer business.

THE 80/20 OF EMPLOYEE TRAINING

"I hated every minute of training, but I said, don't quit. Suffer now and live the rest of your life as a champion."

- Muhammad Ali

PEOPLE LEAVE YOUR COMPANY FOR a lot of reasons - they don't like the work, don't like the boss, or they get a better offer somewhere else. Some things you can control, some things you can't. One area in your control is how well you train employees. If your training program is solid, your employee retention will be solid as well.

Turnover costs money. Some estimates peg the cost at 6 to 9 months of the employee's salary, while others indicate that it is much higher. Based on these estimates, a delivery driver or sales person making $40,000 or $50,000 per year, could cost north of $20,000 to replace.

The cost of employee turnover hurts your income statement, but it also hurts customer service and operations. By improving employee retention, you can avoid these pain points. The 80/20 of employee training will give you the tools needed to train employees so they have the best chance to succeed with your company.

THE 80/20 OF EMPLOYEE TRAINING

- Beware the three little bears of training: too little, too much, and just right.
- Best practices of training: Appeal to the highest level of thinking.
- Use the 80/20 process: Focus on the goal and the vital few.
- Benchmark for success: Use turnover ratios to monitor progress.

THREE LITTLE BEARS OF TRAINING

Throughout my career, I have observed the "three little bears" of training repeatedly: too much, too little, or just the right amount. The first two are deadly for employee turnover.

Too much training occurs when every possible detail about the job responsibilities are jammed into the employee's head on day one – the core job duties, the exceptions, the one-off situations, etc. The "too much trainer" understands the job, but doesn't understand how to simplify and spoon-feed instructions to the employee. The new employee is left bewildered and overwhelmed.

Too little training takes on a different form. In some cases, an employee is hired, shown quickly what to do, and then left on their own. They sink or swim. Usually, they sink.

In other cases, the "too little trainer" plays hide-and-seek with the information. They show the new employee a portion of what they need to know to complete a task, but they leave out a vital step. I've seen this done as deliberate sabotage – the "too little trainer" didn't want the employee to succeed, or the trainer simply wasn't good at communicating the key steps. Either way, the employee loses, and your income statement loses.

Employee turnover costs a lot of money, and bad training is a big reason why.

The goal is to find the "just right" amount of employee training so that your employees have the best chance to succeed with your company. And that's what we'll cover next with the employee training best practices.

EMPLOYEE TRAINING BEST PRACTICES

Dozens of training best practices are out there. Below are the ones I believe are key to giving your employees the best chance at success.

- On-boarding: Start off on the right foot
- Big picture training: What we do and how you make a difference here
- Appeal to the highest level of thinking = Highest level of performance

On-Boarding: Remember that people are overwhelmed the first few weeks on a new job. Everything is new at this stage – new people, names to remember, new routine. Keep it simple, and allow them time to get used to the new environment. Before you bury them in policies and procedures, show them where the bathroom is.

Big Picture Training: In our company, we felt it was important to show employees the big picture of the business. New hires spent an entire day working each part of the operation – sales, merchandising, warehouse, delivery, and admin. This provided an opportunity to experience all aspects of the business and understand how they fit in. People exist to make a difference in the world – Big Picture Training can show them how.

Appeal to the Highest Level of Thinking: This is one of my favorite quotes from Jack Stack, author of the Great Game of Business: "When you appeal to the highest level of thinking, you get the highest level of performance."

Teach employees to think, ask questions, and understand the process of their work. Teach them to see beyond their role and how they fit into the larger mission of the company. Teach them to ask questions: Why am I doing this? What value does this add? How can I improve? When you appeal to the highest level of thinking, employees get engaged. When they are engaged, they have the best chance for success.

THE 80/20 OF EMPLOYEE TRAINING

The 80/20 rule can be applied in every area of your business, including employee training: 20% of activities create 80% of the results. Likewise, you can identify the vital 20% of training that creates 80% of the employee benefit. In other words, identify the result you want and focus your efforts on those training activities that help achieve the result. The concept is a great tool, but it takes time and a thoughtful approach to do it right.

1. Identify the goal – The 80% results you want
2. Identify the training needed to achieve the goal – the 20% effort and where to focus training

For example, if you hire a customer service person, and providing great customer service is the goal, then focus your training here. It sounds obvious, but we often lose sight of the goal when the actual training begins. The customer service job involves computer training, trips to the post office or the bank, and a host of other tasks that are necessary but distract from the primary goal. Connect the goal to training. Identify the 20% training efforts (customer service training, product training) that will get you the 80% results you want (excellence in customer service).

Think of 80/20 training as "training on purpose." Be thoughtful about what the job is and the results you want to achieve. Focus on the aspects that will have the biggest impact to establish a training plan that gives you the best chance to achieve the goal.

WRAP UP AND BENCHMARKS

Measure your progress with 80/20 training by using an employee turnover ratio. Simply divide your average number of total employees by the number of employees that leave the company. If you have 100 employees on average and 10 leave during the year, your annual turnover rate is 10% (10 employee departures divided by 100 average employees).

If you have higher turnover in one department (sales for example), you can measure turnover for just that department. Measure turnover so you can manage and improve.

Employee turnover is expensive. The goal of 80/20 training is to help create successful employees who want to stay with your company. If the employee succeeds, the business succeeds and so does your income statement. Beware the three little bears of training, use the training best practices, and give 80/20 training a try in your company.

COMPENSATION PLANNING BASICS

"Do your job and demand your compensation - but in that order."

-- Cary Grant

IF I WERE TO BOIL down everything I've learned about compensation planning into one sentence, it would be this: Pay your people a market wage and give them a chance to make more if they go above and beyond.

This is the first rule of compensation. Pay a market rate, guarantee it, and pay them more if they exceed their goals. Everything else is just details.

We forget how important it is for people to know what their paycheck is going to be. We all have mortgages, car payments, and groceries to pay for. Salespeople are no different. They need to know the fixed portion of their compensation will cover these basic expenses. They also need to know they have a chance to earn more if they sell more. That's the motivation.

In our company, we tried every conceivable compensation method out there, always in search of the perfect model. Sometimes, we remembered the basic rule of compensation; sometimes, we forgot or got forced off course by a supplier who insisted we pay our sales team a certain way.

Our comp models have included the usual suspects - commissions, pay for performance, base salary, and supplier incentives. We have tweaked the particulars of each item, looking for just the right mix of variable and fixed pay, just the right blend of incentives and security, to achieve the desired result.

The desired result was always the same: to provide Pay That Motivates. The goal was to build a comp plan that provided the desire and motivation for the salesperson to achieve and exceed the company goal, whatever that happened to be at the time.

Sounds like a simple goal, but too often the compensation plans become so convoluted, we create Pay That Confuses. In our zeal to include all the critical objectives, qualifiers, and pay-for-performance items, we over-complicated the plan. The end result was that employees didn't understand how the plan worked or what they needed to do to get paid. Epic fail.

Worse yet, there were times we rolled out a comp model perceived as unfair to the salesperson. The goal was too high, or the calculations weren't well-thought-out. During these times, we created Pay That Infuriates. That's kind of the bottom of the barrel - a comp system that pisses off your sales force. Double epic fail.

During our search for the perfect comp model, we bought several books on sales force incentive compensation. We were looking for ideas to implement to motivate our employees, but what we found were textbooks over 400 pages long. Talk about confusion and over-complication. It really doesn't have to be this difficult.

Let me repeat the first rule of sales compensation: People want a market wage and a chance to make more if they go above and beyond.

I know there are doubters out there. Many folks believe that a 100% commissioned salesperson is the only way to go. I don't agree. I've done hundreds of compensation review meetings with salespeople, and the feedback is always the same: Employees want a steady paycheck, they want to know what to expect so they can pay the bills, and they want to be paid more if they exceed their sales goals. That's it.

But of course, there are the details: the mix of commissions, base salary, pay for performance, and the goals and objectives to achieve. There are also the particulars of the compensation plan design and related calculations. Details are important, but not as important as remembering the first rule of compensation.

COMPENSATION PLANNING CHECKLIST

"I watch a lot of astronaut movies ... mostly Star Wars. And even Han and Chewie use a checklist."

- Jon Stewart

LAST SUMMER I READ THE Checklist Manifesto by Atul Gawande, a doctor who successfully instituted the use of simple checklists to improve outcomes for surgical procedures and virtually eliminate a deadly type of hospital infection that occurs in intensive care units.

The premise is that checklists, while they may be basic and boring, help to ensure that the most important things get done. This fascinating book got me to thinking about how to use them to improve on our business processes.

What I found most striking in the Checklist Manifesto was how often the most important things don't get done – doctors forget to wash their hands, nurses forget to cross-check allergies, anesthesiologists administer the wrong dose, and so on. The checklist, when properly implemented, catches these oversights and prevents the potentially deadly result.

In our beer business, the stakes might not be life and death, but they're pretty important. So, I took a stab at creating a checklist that we beer distributors could use to improve our sales compensation planning. The goal of the checklist isn't to save lives, but to help you remember the most important things when designing your plan. Who knows, maybe it will save a life as well.

THE SALES COMPENSATION PLANNING CHECKLIST

Remember the first rule of compensation: People want security, to be paid a market wage, and want an opportunity to earn more if they go above and beyond. This is the foundation of a good comp plan.

AVOID THESE MISTAKES WHEN DESIGNING YOUR PLAN

- Pay that Confuses: Keep your plan as simple as possible. Confusion costs money. If your employees don't understand how they are paid, they won't achieve the goals.
- Pay that Infuriates: Avoid a comp plan that pisses off your sales force. Design the plan, share it with key sales people in advance, get their input, and iron out any irritation.
- Pay that Surprises: Don't play hide-and-seek with the reward. If there's a bonus or incentive at stake, tell the sales person what it is and how to win it.

BE INTENTIONAL WITH YOUR MODEL

Are you paying for process, outcome, or both?

- Process: Paying people to do things in a certain way, to follow the script or the checklist. Even McDonald's wants employees to follow the script - don't ad lib with the fries. You may want sales people to follow a specific sales call process.
- Outcome: Paying people to achieve things, such as increased sales or placements. Think of Alec Baldwin in Glengarry Glen Ross: "Put. That. Coffee. Down! Coffee is for closers." No sale, no commission. No coffee.
- Process and Outcome: Many companies have a blend of both in the comp plan.

Bottom line: Be intentional with your plan and determine whether you want to pay for following a process or achieving an outcome.

USE INCENTIVES WISELY; THEY ARE SUPER POWERS

With great power comes great responsibility. Incentives work, but design them properly using the SMART method: specific, measurable, agreed-upon, realistic, and time-based. It's not rocket science, it just works.

MAKE THE SALESPERSON KEEP SCORE

Everyone has an iPad to connect to the sales data. Invest in training the salesperson to run their own reports and see where they stand related to their goals. You don't want to come up short because they didn't know the score.

ALIGN THE COMPENSATION PLAN WITH COMPANY GOALS FIRST

In a perfect world, the goals of your company and the goals of your suppliers will be the same. But in this imperfect world, that's not always the case. Review, acknowledge and incorporate supplier goals into your comp planning. However, if push comes to shove, put a priority on your company goals first.

DON'T FORGET COACHING, MANAGING, AND LEADING

Your comp model can't do it alone – you need to be there to cheer on the team. Coaching, managing, and leading your employees are vital to a successful comp plan.

COMMUNICATE AND PROVIDE EDUCATION ON THE PLAN – THEN REPEAT

You'd think people would pay close attention when it comes to understanding how they are paid. They don't. Tell them in spoken words, hand them written words, field questions, and repeat.

CONCLUSION

Checklists are basic and can be boring, but they accomplish an amazing result - they help us remember the most important things. In a busy world with emails, texts, phone calls, and a myriad of other distractions, it's helpful to slow down and focus. Checklists help us do just that.

When designing your sales comp plan, slow down and use the checklist to remember the most important things. Your sales team will thank you.

WRAP UP

ACTION ITEMS

List any ideas from this section that can help improve financial results in your beer business.

Write down an action plan: How and when to implement the idea.

Do it now before you forget or get busy with something else. Your income statement is counting on you.

- ☐ ____________________
- ☐ ____________________
- ☐ ____________________
- ☐ ____________________
- ☐ ____________________
- ☐ ____________________
- ☐ ____________________
- ☐ ____________________
- ☐ ____________________
- ☐ ____________________

WHOLESALER OPERATIONS

INTRODUCTION TO WHOLESALER OPERATIONS

EVERYTHING THAT HAPPENS IN YOUR beer business to keep it running smoothly and earning money is known collectively as operations. In particular, wholesaler operations consist of selling, delivering, and warehousing activities.

Managing human resources, administration, information technology, and customer service are other important components of wholesaler operations as well. And of course, let's not forget finance and accounting. In short, hundreds of tasks, decisions, and responsibilities fall under the operations umbrella.

In this chapter we'll focus on four specific areas of wholesaler operations:

- Out of code beer: How to manage and reduce this growing expense.
- Lease vs; buy: How to determine which is the best financial choice for your beer business.

- Workplace safety: A system you can use to improve safety and accountability for your employees.
- Asset tracking: Wholesalers have a lot of expensive assets. Use our process to help keep track of everything.

We'll look at the numbers, costs, and options related to each topic. Additionally, we'll look at a simple process you can use to reduce costs and make better financial decisions in your beer business.

HOW TO MANAGE OUT OF CODE BEER

"Smell the cheese often so you know when it's getting old."
- Spencer Johnson, Who Moved My Cheese?

OUT OF CODE BEER IS an expensive problem for beer distributors. And the problem is growing with the rapid increase of new breweries, brands and packages. Lurking in the shadows of this beer nirvana is a ticking time bomb for beer distributors: old beer on the shelves.

Old beer is a problem for beer distributors because they bear the full burden of dealing with it. The stale, dated product must be identified, removed from the retail account, and destroyed, with all the cost on the distributor's dime.

The key is to identify old beer before it goes bad and have a plan in place to get it sold to the consumer while the beer is still fresh.

In this section we'll reveal the total costs of old beer and share a process you can use to reduce this growing cost in your beer business.

- Know the rules: How to read the code dates
- The cost of out of code beer: It's more than you may think
- Implement and follow this close code process
- Track, measure, and monitor to reduce out of code in your beer business

KNOW THE RULES: HOW TO READ THE CODE DATES

Like many consumer products, beer comes with a code date that indicates the shelf life of the product. Generally speaking, package beer has a shelf life of 90 to 180 days and draft beer is good for 60 days. These dates assume the beer is treated properly, refrigerated, and kept out of direct sunlight. Any mistreatment can significantly shorten the actual shelf life.

Code dates on beer are notoriously difficult to decipher. Some breweries use a Best By date, which is straight-forward. The beer is good until the date indicated. Other breweries use a Born-On date. This is helpful, but only if you know how long the beer should be good for. Still, other breweries use a Julian dating system or their own proprietary system.

The range of code date systems, combined with the varying shelf life of different beers, makes it a difficult task to identify close coded beer.

To hone in on close coded beer, you need to be able to read and understand the code dates. Start by assembling a comprehensive list of the breweries, brands, and packages with their related code dates.

If you can't figure out the dates on your own, insist that your supplier partners provide code date information for their products.

THE COST OF OLD BEER

Old beer costs a lot more than you may think. On average, for every one case of beer that goes out of code, the distributor must sell five cases to make up for it.

When beer goes out of code, it must be removed from the retail account (or warehouse) and destroyed. The retailer gets a credit for the old beer, while the cost and responsibility for removal are borne by the beer distributor. And the costs add up fast.

The many cost components of out of code beer are as follows:

- Cost of the beer (often referred to as the FOB cost)
- Cost of freight - the amount paid to the freight carrier when the beer was originally received
- Cost to pick up the old beer from the retailer and bring back to the warehouse (delivery time, warehouse time, administrative time)
- Cost to destroy the product (shipping and destruction fees)

Results may vary and the specific costs will differ from distributor to distributor. However, it takes a lot of new sales to make up for every case of beer that goes out of code.

Run the numbers for your operation and determine your actual costs. Use an average cost per case so that it is easy to communicate the financial impact of every case of out of code beer.

When we first did this exercise in our distribution company, a lot of people were surprised. They had no idea how much old beer cost the company. This knowledge, combined with an increased awareness of the problem of managing old beer, helped to get our teams engaged to reduce the expense. It worked for us; it can work for you as well.

IMPLEMENT A CLOSE CODE PROCESS

It takes a village to reduce out of code beer and the related expense that hits your income statement.

Drivers and merchandisers must properly rotate product at retail to ensure the older code dates are sold first. The warehouse team needs to do the same in the warehouse – ensuring older beer is rotated to the front of the line so that loaders pick it first. Everyone has a role in reducing old beer expense.

You can use the example close code process outlined below as a template to reduce old beer in your company. As with any process, it only works if you communicate the plan, educate your team on how it works, and insist on following the plan.

Important Note: Regulations vary from market to market. Make sure you comply with relevant state and federal regulations, and use the ideas presented only where legal to do so.

1. Identify Close Code Product
    - Identify, remove, and send back product with 30 to 45 days of shelf life remaining to the warehouse for distribution to an account where it has a better chance of being sold.

2. Segregate Close Code Product
    - Store the product in a separately marked area of the warehouse so that the warehouse and night crew can locate and pick from this close coded product.

3. Communicate Close Code Product on Hand
    - The warehouse counts the Close Code product every Friday and sends a list to the salesman by email so they know the details going into a new week.

4. Identify Accounts That Turn Product Faster
    - Each sales rep should provide at least three accounts that can turn Close Code product quickly. This creates a target list to sell to.

5. Sell the Close Code Product
    - Sales team will request Close Code product go to accounts where it has the best chance to sell – high volume accounts, for example. The night team will also use their discretion and send it to pre-designated accounts.

6. Communicate Where Close Code is Sold.
    - Send a weekly report to the sales team showing the close code product sold by account.

REDUCE OUT OF CODE

Once the Close Code Process is on paper and communicated to your team, you'll need a method to determine if it's actually working. The mission is to reduce out of code beer expense, plain and simple.

Use a spreadsheet to track progress. Set the goal in cases, dollars or both. Track actual old beer against the goal. Communicate and send updates regularly so the team can see the results.

As an alternative to the spreadsheet, most route accounting software should be able to produce an Out of Code Beer report. It should provide all the details about the old beer: package, account, quantity, sales rep, team leader, etc.

Look for trends in the data. Does one sales rep have significantly more old beer than the others? Are there particular packages or brands that stand out? Are there certain retail accounts that have a lot more old beer than others?

Bottom line: Keep it simple. Set a goal to reduce old beer, keep track of actual losses, and report the results regularly to your team.

WRAP UP

Out of code beer is growing expense for beer distributors. With so many new breweries, brands, and packages it can be difficult to stay on top of all the code dates on beer. But that's your job.

Use the process presented here or develop one that works better for your company. Communicate the plan, educate your team on what needs to be done, and insist that they follow the process. Afterward, track, measure, and monitor old beer to make sure the process is working.

In short, old beer is bad for everyone. Do your part to reduce it.

THE LEASE VS. BUY DECISION

"We are only tenants, and shortly the great Landlord will give us notice that our lease has expired."

-- Joseph Jefferson

THE AGE-OLD QUESTION REGARDING YOUR truck fleet is whether it makes more sense to lease or buy. The age-old answer is that it depends: One, it depends on your fleet size, the type of trucks you run, and your appetite and ability to maintain them; two, it depends on your ability to negotiate good lease terms or your ability to come up with a down payment on the purchase of a truck; and three, it depends on how long you plan on using the truck and how many miles you intend to drive.

In this section we will dig into each of the above set of factors. Let's get into two broad answers to the question of leasing or buying:

1. Quantitatively, by studying the numbers and financial aspects of each option
2. Qualitatively, by considering business factors other than numbers

THE NUMBERS

In my experience, from a purely financial standpoint, it makes more sense to buy your trucks. You own the asset and retain the equity in the vehicle. The cost of financing of a truck is almost always going to be less than the monthly lease cost.

However, you also have the obligation to maintain the asset, which is where you can run into headaches. Trucks require regular service; sometimes, they break down on the side of the road and require road calls, on-site repairs, or towing. The cost of maintenance can be significant.

To run the analysis on the numbers, compare the financial elements of the lease terms to a purchase:

- Lease: This means paying the base lease cost and cents-per-mile maintenance charge. The base lease cost, a fixed amount you pay each month, won't change, whether you drive the truck 100 miles or 10,000. The cents-per-mile charge is variable and covers the cost of maintenance. The good news is that you'll know exactly how much maintenance will cost you. The bad news is that every mile you drive, the expense meter keeps running.
- Buy: The means paying the cost of financing a new truck and estimated internal cost per mile for maintenance. The former depends on a variety of factors: cost of the vehicle, amount of the down payment required, interest rate, and loan term. The cost of financing is always less than the base lease cost you'll pay to the leasing company.

So that leads us to the key differentiator: the variable fleet maintenance cost. The key question to ask and answer is: How much does it cost you to maintain your own trucks?

If you have owned trucks previously and have a record of your maintenance and expense records, the calculation should be easy. Simply divide total maintenance costs by total miles driven. You can use a one-year period, two years, etc. The longer the better, because you'll be comparing this average cost per mile to the cents-per-mile maintenance cost from the leasing company. Maintenance costs fluctuate – fewer costs with a newer truck, more costs with an older one – so it's helpful to compare your own historical costs over a longer period of time.

Lease vs Buy Analysis						
	Lease Cost					
	Total Trucks	Variable Per Mile	Estimated Miles/Yr	Annual Variable Costs	Annual Fixed Costs	Extended Total Costs Year
Tractor	1	$0.078	12,000	$936	$21,736	$22,672
Single Axle no Liftgate (33k GVW)	1	$0.075	16,000	$1,200	$15,340	$16,540
Single Axle w/ Liftgate (33k GVW)	1	$0.075	16,000	$1,200	$17,836	$19,036
Tandem Axle w/Liftgate	1	$0.085	19,000	$1,615	$21,892	$23,507
Totals	4		63,000	$4,951	$76,804	**$81,755**

FACTORS OTHER THAN NUMBERS

> *"The core concept of a full-service lease option is that we (leasing companies) are in the fleet maintenance business, and our customers are not, and they shouldn't be. Outsourcing their fleet to a full-service lease provider allows clients to free up executive talent within their organization for more productive functions."*
>
> *– Jon Dumas, Ryder Transportation*

We have worked with Ryder for many years to structure our truck leases. The quote above from Jon Dumas nicely sums up the qualitative benefits of a lease arrangement: Leasing companies are in the fleet maintenance business. On the other hand, beer companies are in the business of selling and delivering beer, so in many respects, it makes sense to partner up and allow each company to do what they do best.

From a qualitative standpoint, the key factors in the lease vs. buy decision process come down to asking yourself a few basic questions: Do you want to deal with maintenance issues on your trucks? Do you want to deal with truck downtime, road calls, and the hassles that go along with keeping a machine running?

If you answered no to the questions above, a full-service lease can eliminate these headaches. A full-service lease gets you peace of mind and predictability: your truck fleet will be taken care of, and you'll have a trusted business partner by your side to help you when equipment breaks down. A professional leasing service company will handle all maintenance issues, provide a spare truck when needed, and conduct any road calls to deal with break-downs.

DECISION TIME: LEASE OR BUY?

In our company we have worked with both lease and buy scenarios for our truck fleet. In a nutshell, I prefer to own and maintain. Operationally, it was cumbersome, but financially it was significantly better than the lease scenario.

When we owned, we had the benefit of a full-time, on-site mechanic. He would keep the trucks well-maintained and do road-calls if a truck broke down during a delivery. An owned-fleet with a full-time mechanic worked very well for us, financially and operationally.

When our mechanic retired, we closed down the garage and transitioned to a leased fleet of trucks. The relationship with our leasing partners was good. The lease terms, service levels, and overall relationship was mixed though.

In the end, I prefer to own and control our own assets. It is debatable whether time, energy, and money spent on owning and maintaining a truck fleet is the best use of resources, but in our case, I believe it was.

Do the analysis and determine the financial components of the lease vs. buy equation. Understand what you are getting into with a lease contract – fixed costs, variable costs, length of commitment. Also, understand the costs of ownership and make your best estimates on the costs to maintain your trucks.

FOUR STEPS TO IMPROVE SAFETY, AND SAVE MONEY

> *"Every accident is a notice that something is wrong with men, methods, or material. Investigate. Then act."*
>
> *- Safety saying, circa early 1900s*

THE BEER BUSINESS IS LABOR intensive. Warehouse employees are constantly lifting, twisting, turning, and loading trucks. Drivers are wheeling kegs down ramps, and merchandisers are lifting cases and stocking shelves. Every time one of your employees picks something up, they risk an injury - and you risk a workers comp claim.

On average, workers comp insurance costs about 3% of total payroll expense. For a beer distributor with $10 million in payroll, that works out to $300,000 per year in premiums.

A focus on safety says you care about your employees. It also says you care about your P&L. After all, establishing a safety and accountability plan can help reduce accidents, lost time due to injury, and expenses on your income statement. Everyone wins.

On the surface, the term safety and accountability plan sounds like a real yawner. But stay with me as we walk through the steps. There's real value to help your employees and your bottom line.

Four Steps to Improved Safety

1. File the report, but don't stop there.
2. Injury follow up: What happened and how can we prevent it?
3. Accountability follow up: Everyone is responsible for safety, especially the employee.
4. Observation and reporting of unsafe actions: Prevent injuries from happening in the first place.

Step 1: File the first report of injury. This is the step that starts the claims process. A member of human resources speaks with the injured employee to find out what happened, gather basic facts and details, and fill out the form. The employee is then referred to medical attention, if needed. This standard procedure covers the basic requirements.

In our safety and accountability plan, we suggest you take this basic requirement a few steps further. Question the details of the incident and determine if the incident was preventable. Ask some probing questions: How did the incident occur? What could have been done to prevent the injury? What could we do better as a company to better protect our employees and avoid an injury like this from reoccurring?

Lastly, alert senior management to the incident. The "tone from the top" is critical when implementing the safety plan. If ownership and upper management are aware of incidents and actively involved in understanding what happened, everyone's attention is heightened. For a safety plan to be taken seriously, it has to be understood that it is important. If ownership is paying attention, it's important.

Step 2: Injury follow-up. Within 24 hours of the incident, the employee should have had an appointment with the medical facility (if needed) as well as received a note regarding restrictions, a treatment plan, and a follow-up appointment. Human resources reviews this information and works with the general manager or team supervisor on a work plan. Again, this is the standard process for many beer distributors, but take it to another level with the next step.

Step 3: Accountability follow-up. Here's where the magic happens. This is the deep dive into what happened, what caused the injury, and most importantly, how can it be prevented in the future.

If the incident occurred due to unsafe work conditions, human resources will contact the general manager and discuss the circumstances immediately. An action plan to fix the unsafe conditions will be created and implemented within 24 hours of the incident.

If the incident occurred due to the employee's unsafe actions, the team leader, general manager, and human resources will meet with the employee within one week of the incident and discuss what happened to determine the sequence of events and how incidents like can be prevented in the future. Ask questions like:

- What could the employee have done differently to prevent the injury?
- What can we do better as a company to prevent this type of injury from reoccurring?
- Does the employee need additional training or re-training on tasks to perform their job duties in a safe manner?

Based on the answers, the employee may be subject to disciplinary action up to and including termination. This is tough love. Nobody wants to get hurt, but sometimes employees do dumb things and injure themselves. It costs them time away from work, and it costs the company money in increased insurance premiums.

Step 4: Observation and reporting of unsafe actions. This is the proactive portion of the safety plan – working to stop injuries before they actually happen.

How often have you seen an employee reach over a pallet to pick up a case? How often has one of your supervisors seen a driver hop out of the cab of a truck without abiding by the three-points of contact rule? It happens all the time.

The safety plan mandates that these actions require the same level of scrutiny as any incident or injury. If an owner, member of senior management, or team leader observes unsafe actions, it warrants a meeting between the employee and the GM, human resources, and immediate supervisor to understand out the circumstances and hold the employee accountable.

WRAP UP

Practicing safety says you care. Sometimes, it requires a little tough love, accountability, and getting called on the carpet. Your employees may not like it, but the plan will help them stay safe. It will also help out your income statement by reducing expenses in lower workers comp premiums and less lost time due to injury. Follow the four steps above to implement a safety and accountability plan in your beer company today.

THE ASSET TRACKING SYSTEM

"One of the great responsibilities that I have is to manage my assets wisely so that they create value."

- Alice Walton

DISTRIBUTORS LIKE YOU HAVE A lot of expensive assets; warehouses, trucks, and equipment can add up to millions or tens of millions of dollars. However, do you have a good system to keep track of and manage your assets so that they create value?

In this section, we'll review best practices for tracking and safeguarding your assets. We'll look at how to use asset tags and fixed asset software so you become confident that all your assets are properly recorded on the books.

How to Track your Fixed Assets:

- Fixed Asset Best Practices
- How to Use Asset tags
- The Basics of Fixed Asset Software to track your Stuff

FIXED ASSET BASICS

Assets are the things you own: cars, trucks, and warehouse equipment, for instance. The term Fixed Assets simply means the asset will last a long time. They are recorded on your balance sheet along with your liabilities and equity.

When you buy a new delivery truck, for example, the amount of the purchase is recorded on your balance sheet as an asset. Any additional costs to get the equipment up and running are included in the value of the asset.

As new fixed assets are purchased, they are added to the balance sheet. It divides them into suitable categories. Leasehold improvements, for example, might include the cost of additions and upgrades to the warehouse over several years.

The balance sheet provides a summary of the type of fixed assets owned and the total cost in each category. The fixed asset schedule displays all the asset details.

Example of Assets section of Balance Sheet		
Fixed Assets		
1605-00	Warehouse	$1,250,000
1610-00	Leasehold Improvements	$350,000
1615-00	Warehouse Equipment	$120,000
1620-00	Office Equipment	$75,000
1625-00	Sales Vehicles	$150,000
1630-00	Delivery Trucks	$450,000
		$2,395,000

FIXED ASSET BEST PRACTICES

The first best practice is to create a policy for fixed assets, i.e., a set of rules that determine how you purchase and record your fixed assets. It serves as a road map your team can use to properly account for your assets.

The fixed asset policy should include the following items:

- Rules to define fixed assets. For example, asset purchases over $5,000 that will last more than a year are recorded as fixed assets on the balance sheet.
- Rules for purchasing. Any spend over $5,000 requires at least two competitive quotes and approval from the General Manager prior to committing to the spend.
- Fixed assets will be counted and reconciled on an annual basis, just like with a physical count of your finished goods inventory.
- Disposition or sale of fixed assets. When an asset is sold or scrapped, the fixed asset listing and balance sheet will be updated to account for the transaction.

The next best practice is to keep a file of all invoice copies when equipment is purchased. Place them in a separate file (electronic or old-fashioned). This way, you'll have a complete list when it comes time to update your fixed assets and depreciation schedules (more on this later).

Afterward, test your fixed assets for completeness and accuracy, two terms accountants love. They help ensure your fixed assets are properly recorded.

More specifically, completeness means that the fixed asset listing shows everything you own. To test this, walk the warehouse, identify a fixed asset, then locate it on the listing. If you can't find it, the asset list may be incomplete.

On the other hand, accuracy means that items on the fixed asset listing actually exist. Very often, assets are sold or scrapped, and the listing is not updated. To test this, take the asset listing and look for the physical assets in the warehouse. This is like a game of hide-and-seek. Hopefully, your assets come out to play.

TRACKING SYSTEMS: ASSET TAGS

Asset tags come in all shapes and sizes. Inexpensive and easy to use, most are heavyweight stickers with a strong adhesive so they don't peel off. They have a unique barcode you can scan to count and identify items. The idea is to stick them on every fixed asset item you want to track - warehouse equipment, computers, printers, and even office furniture.

The asset tag number on the equipment will be the same number on the fixed asset listing, making it easy to check for completeness and accuracy. You can also use it to track equipment if it moves from one location to another. For example, if you have multiple warehouses and equipment is moved from one location to another.

FIXED ASSET SOFTWARE

Once you have your fixed asset best practices on paper and asset tags on your equipment, it's time to install software to automate the process. We use Fixed Assets CS software from Thomson Reuters to track all the asset details, including:

- Asset groups: Equipment, vehicles, improvements, etc.
- Asset number: the number on the asset tag
- Description of the asset
- Date in service: date asset was purchased and placed in service
- Cost: purchase price
- Depreciation expense: current and prior depreciation expense
- Net book value: asset's net value (cost minus total depreciation expense)
- Tax period: the useful life of the asset, such as five years for a new truck
- Tax method: accounting mumbo jumbo that tells you how the asset is depreciated. For example, straight-line depreciation expenses the asset evenly over its useful life.

Don't get lost in the details; just know that good depreciation software can make tracking your fixed assets easier.

WRAP UP + ACTION ITEMS

As a distributor, you'll have invested a lot of money in equipment. Therefore, make sure you invest in a fixed asset process to safeguard and properly track all those assets.

First, develop a fixed asset policy or borrow from the one listed above. This simple set of rules will guide purchasing decisions and management of your assets.

Then, invest in asset tags for your equipment. These barcode stickers make asset tracking a piece of cake. They are inexpensive and easy to apply.

Afterward, invest in fixed asset software to keep all your asset details in one place. Your accountants will appreciate this as well.

Now, get out there and track those assets. Your financial statements are counting on you.

WRAP UP

ACTION ITEMS

List any ideas from this section that can help improve financial results in your beer business.

Write down an action plan: How and when to implement the idea.

Do it now before you forget or get busy with something else. Your income statement is counting on you.

- ☐ ______________________________
- ☐ ______________________________
- ☐ ______________________________
- ☐ ______________________________
- ☐ ______________________________
- ☐ ______________________________
- ☐ ______________________________
- ☐ ______________________________
- ☐ ______________________________
- ☐ ______________________________

WRAP UP + ACTION ITEMS

WITH THE BEER BUSINESS BECOMING more competitive day by day, a solid understanding of your financial numbers gives you a competitive advantage. This does not have to involve fancy accounting; it's just about using numbers to make better decisions.

In this book, we cover a lot of financial ground, including an introduction to beer finance, the basics of financial reporting, and much more. More specifically, this book is a summary of the many things I learned during a transition from one generation of beer wholesaler ownership to the next. The pages hold the ideas, tactics, and strategies that proved not only useful but also profitable as our business grew. I've shared ideas that worked and ideas that didn't so that you can learn from our successes and failures.

Overall, we covered:

- Strategies to grow sales in a hyper-competitive market
- Tools to manage and improve wholesaler gross profit
- Specific ideas and tactics to reduce operating expenses
- Templates and spreadsheet models to monitor and improve cash flow and profitability

The methods presented are ones I've used in the real world to help improve financial results our beer business, and I hope they will do the same for you. The information is here, and the financial benefits to your beer business are clear. The next move is up to you. How will you put this knowledge to use?

ABOUT THE AUTHOR

KARY SHUMWAY is the founder of Beer Business Finance and Craft Brewery Finance, online resources for beer industry professionals. Shumway has worked in the beer industry for more than 20 years as a Certified Public Accountant, chief financial officer for a beer distributor, and currently as CFO for Wormtown Brewery in Worcester, MA.

Beer Business Finance publishes a weekly finance newsletter for beer wholesalers. Guide books and courses are available on topics such as sales compensation planning, financial training for non-financial managers and tactics to reduce out of code beer expense. The newsletter with a free trial, industry guides and resources are available at www.BeerBusinessFinance.com

REVIEWS FOR BEER BUSINESS FINANCE:
A Handbook for the Next Generation Beer Wholesaler

"When I graduated from the University of Texas, my father was horrified to find that he had paid for four years of study and an economics degree and I somehow still didn't learn how to read financial statements. A balance sheet? It was Greek to me. Gross profit? Sounded like something disgusting.

"I sure wish I had Kary's book back then, as it would've saved me a lot of confusion and embarrassment. Being literate in finance is crucial even if you are in sales, and Kary has laid it down in an easy-to-read and simple manner. I will even make my artist son read it."

Harry Schuhmacher, editor and publisher, Beer Business Daily

"Kary does an exceptionally fine job of highlighting the issues facing distributors today and with his extensive background, he knows how it impacts the bottom-line of operating a distribution business. I always look forward to reading his updates and continue to learn from his vast depth of real-life expertise."

Bump Williams, BWC Consulting

"Kary's new book is like a distributor-focused MBA. A must read for your entire management team."

John Conlin, Beverage Business Consultant

"This book delivers practical and straightforward financial advice for beer distributors. It is a great guide to the important blocking and tackling of beer business finances and management."

Scott Sadowsky, President, Williams Distributing

"I've had the good fortune of working shoulder to shoulder with Kary Shumway for the last 16 years. I can tell you, unequivocally, that Kary is a man of the highest integrity with the intellect and financial acumen to match. Kary helped guide a 3rd generation family business through multiple acquisitions, integrations and ultimately helped our family sell our businesses while maximizing its value.

"He is a very thoughtful decision maker and his decisions are usually based on the numbers. We all know the numbers don't lie and Kary evaluates that better than anyone I have ever worked with. It is my great honor to highly recommend Beer Business Finance to anyone who wants to increase their bottom line."

Rich Clarke, former President, Clarke Distributors, Inc.

"Am I properly managing keg inventory? How do I build a safety program? How do I manage cash flow? Just ask Kary Shumway. He has an answer and also a real gift for simplifying the beer business with solutions you can easily put into action."

Keith Gribbins, editor, Craft Brewing Business.

"Kary's book neatly condenses decades of learning and insights into an easy-to-read and entertaining executive summary of distributor finances that can only come with decades of hands on experience in the industry. A worthwhile read for all managers/executives of any distributor discipline or department as it smartly summarizes functional learning and seamlessly folds finances into one's macro understanding of distributor operations. Probability is high that you'll save your business some money when your team reads the book."

Scott Schaier, Executive Director,
New Hampshire Beverage Distributors Association

"Over the years, I've worked alongside Kary to develop numerous deep dives for Brewbound.com on topics such as understanding taproom-focused business models, and the economics of self-distribution, among others. Kary has a deep understanding of the beer business and his handbook on understanding the financial side of an incredibly complex industry is an excellent resource for anyone interested in operating their wholesale business more profitably. "

Chris Furnari, Editor, Brewbound

"If you are like me, you spent your formative years under the impression that sales would drive profits and profits would pay the bills. Beer Business Finance is the cliff notes version of an MBA in financial management I wish I had 20 years ago. Shumway applies real world, street level distributor financial principles to the beer business that will simply make you a more complete manager and help you apply sound financial decisions to all aspects of your beer distribution business."

David Fields, former President, Consolidated Beverages

"Kary Shumway has written a book that needs to be read by everyone in the beer industry. Beer Business Finance will be the new go-to book that will put beer companies on the best solid financial footing and give ownership guidance on many critical decisions for years to come. One thing that will echo throughout the beer world after reading this book is that it's all in the numbers, baby!

Jay Clarke, former Executive Vice President, Clarke Companies

FURTHER READING:

Financial Intel for Beer Distributors

Thank you for taking the time to read this book. It has been a pleasure sharing my work with you.

If you enjoyed *Beer Business Finance, A Handbook for the Next Generation Beer Wholesaler*, then you may like my other writing as well. My latest articles are sent out in my weekly newsletter. Subscribers are the first to hear about my newest online courses, guide books, and spreadsheet templates. All the materials are designed to help beer distributors improve financial results in their beer business.

Free Bonus only for readers of this book: Use the discount code **NBWA Book** at checkout to save 15% off the annual subscription to Beer Business Finance.

Learn more at www.BeerBusinessFinance.com.

Made in the USA
Columbia, SC
15 April 2019